The Kingsto…

Mary Caine

CAPALL BANN PUBLISHING

www.capallbann.co.uk

The Kingston Zodiac

ISBN 186163 1111

Cover design by Paul Mason

Published by:

Capall Bann Publishing
Freshfields
Chieveley
Berks
RG20 8TF

Contents

By the same author, also published by Capall Bann:

The Celtic Saints and the Glastonbury Zodiac

A Kingston Zodiac
Scale ½" : 1 mile
HANWELL CAPRICORN
CHISWICK
KEW
PUTNEY
WANDSWORTH
R. THAMES
SCORPIO
SAGITTARIUS
WIMBLEDON
MERTON
KINGSTON
LIBRA
SURBITON
HAM
TEDDINGTON
HAMPTON COURT
DITTON
SUTTON
VIRGO
BANSTEAD
EWELL
EPSOM
LEATHERHEAD
LEO
MOLESEY
TWINS
CANCER
WALTON
WEYBRIDGE
OSTERLEY
HESTON
PISCES
HANWORTH
ARIES
ASHFORD
TAURUS
STAINES
EGHAM
CHERTSEY
COBHAM COMMON
GUARD DOG

KINGSTON ZODIAC
How the Planisphere corresponds
when its stars are reflected on earth, or
reversed to scale on the map.

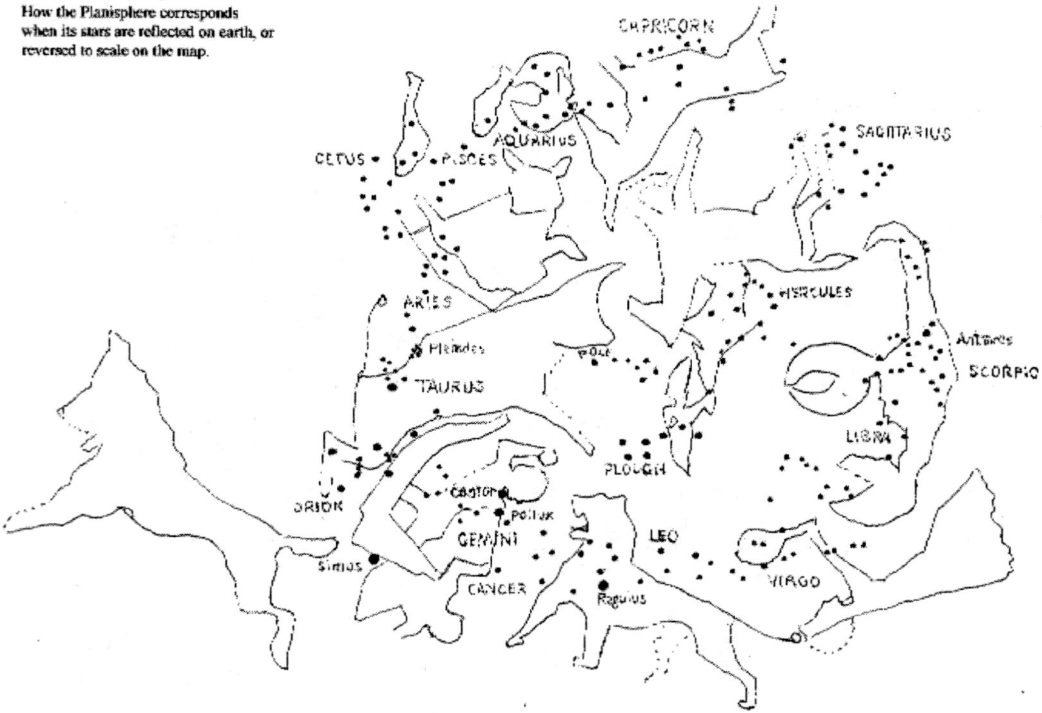

Introduction

KINGSTON-ON-THAMES can't compare with Glastonbury as a Mecca for Grail-questers; long-haired idealists don't play guitars in Richmond Park or wash their jeans in Wolsey's well houses in Coombe Hill.

Shepperton has forgotten its Good Shepherd just across the river; Sunbury's sun-god has been buried too long. Who now remembers Esher's Jesus, or sees Syon Park as footing the Hill of Zion, or realises that the Roman Stane Street runs past the Virgin of Nonsuch, just as the Fosse Way goes past Somerset's Virgo?

A Zodiac round Kingston? Too much! It was my reaction too, at first. But a perceptive friend, intrigued by the town's unique Coronation Stone and the Zodiacal names of its pubs, suggested that as I lived there the least I could do was investigate with an open mind. (I was at the time writing on the Glastonbury Zodiac and wanted to finish that first, but couldn't help noticing those pub names - Ram, Bull, Red Lion, White Hart, Griffin, Druid's Head, North Star, Three Pigeons, etc.) Some of these old names have now changed for the worse, in the current fashion for renaming them; but I remembered too that Kingston once had an inn called the Sun.

The Zodiac is the sun' s path through the sky; the sun is the hero of all its myths - the twelve Houses the scene of his birth, exploits, death and resurrection - the hidden fount of all ancient religions. (Adam-Sagittarius, Eve-Virgo, Cain and Abel their sons, are arguably one such myth. Seen thus, Kingston's Eden Street, Apple-Market, serpentine Thames and its vanished Adam and Eve Inn appeared in a new light.) And when I read Biden's History of Kingston and found that the town's oldest legend sounded like sun-myth, interest

Above, the Old Parish Church at Kingston and, below, the King's Stone.

began to mount. And what a lofty excuse for a pub-crawl! Kingston's footballers should remember this legend.

It appears in abbreviated form in the Anglo-Saxon Chronicle. King Kenwhal, about 755 AD, was lured to Merton by love of its fair maid, and there killed by his cousin Kynard. Kenwhal's incensed followers marched to Merton and decapitated his killer, kicking his head all the way back to Kingston. A ghastly football game ensued in the Market, using the two bridges as goals. This became an annual Hocktide custom, with a ball replacing the original head, growing more and more riotous until the last century - when the town's burghers, tired of broken windows, banished the contestants to a field outside the town centre where they could do less damage. Thus the Kingstonian Football Club began.

Sun-kings in myth are betrayed by love, killed by a jealous relative or trusted follower; Caradoc was betrayed to the Romans by his cousin Cartismandua, Arthur betrayed by Guinevere and his trusted knight Lancelot, killed by his nephew-son Mordred; Osiris killed by his own brother, Set; Adam betrayed by Eve... Does Kingston remember when Biblical and solar myth were one?

Kenwhal and Kynard, Richard of Cirencester tells us, descended from Cerdic. But so did Alfred a century or two later - some of his descendants were crowned on our Coronation Stone, his son Edward the Elder being the first name inscribed upon it. But was Kenwhal crowned here long before? He is real enough, though like many early heroes he acquired mythical legends.

It is notable that Kingston's Wessex kings were closely connected with Glastonbury; Kenwhal was the first Saxon to conquer that area, but revered its Abbey, leaving its British abbot in place. Edward the Elder's son is buried there;

Edmund Hill being named after him.Two Saxon palaces bounded the Zodiac, though neither have survived - one to the south at Somerton, Edgar's, named after him to the north at Edgarley, under the Tor. Dunstan who crowned some of these kings at Kingston, was a Glastonbury native, born at Baltonsborough on Sagittarius and a choirboy at the Abbey. Bard and bishop in one, his harp always slung on his back as he traversed England from west to east, he loved the old Celtic songs; and as he was also reputed to be an alchemist - that is, in the Mysteries - he must have known of the Glastonbury Zodiac. In fact it is from a contemporary Life of this saint that we first get a glimpse of it as '*an ancient church there not made with human hands, but built by the heavens themselves for the salvation of men*' Another version says it was built by the Lord Himself, and this has led to speculation that Jesus Himself built the first little church in Glastonbury when according to local legend he came as a boy with his tin-trading uncle Joseph of Arimathea to Britain. It was called 'the Ealde Kirke' and was made of wattle and daub.But it seems more likely that the enigmatic phrases ' the heavens themselves' and ' the Lord Himself ' refer to a Divine origin of the *Zodiac* - for it is indeed a mirror-image of the stars laid out on earth.

These Zodiacs are basically natural, being contoured and thus partly outlined by rivers; they are too large to be primarily human handiwork; and though the effigy outlines are completed by roads and paths these too have responded to Nature's dictates. Old settlements for instance were only possible where there was a reliable water-supply, and roads between them had to find a ford to cross a river. Katharine Maltwood, the sculptress who discovered or rediscovered the Glastonbury Zodiac in the 1920s, surmised that its basic pattern was recognised and developed by Sumerians, coming here in search of metals roundabout 2700 BC. And startling though this theory may seem, several of the effigies have been built up with earthworks and mounds of this period, while others have been outlined by streams and canals. Sumerians were great astrologers and irrigators , and Glastonbury Tor with its great terraces resembles nothing so much as one of their Ziggurats.

Dunstan was not the first Druidic bishop to the Saxon kings; the name of St Swithin, Alfred's mentor, implies that he was of the Sywedydd - Druids. He is still credited with Druidic powers over the weather! And Alfred, now; did he know of Glastonbury' s Zodiac? For he was on the Guard-Dog's nose when, as his biographer Asser tells us, he burnt those cakes at Athelney. Katharine Maltwood suspected that those burnt cakes were no accident, but a sop to Cerberus dropped into the dog's tongue, the river Tone, by Alfred as an initiate seeking admission to its mysteries. Burnt barley cakes figured in Celtic rituals. There's no doubt about this Hound; some twenty-five place-names remember him, including Wagg on his tail, Earlake Moor on his ear, and numerous Cur-names like Curload, Curland and Curry Rivell nearby. Starsland Farm lies three miles west of his nose, and Somerset's old Wassail song also refers to him as the 'Girt Dog of Langport.'

Kingston and its kings are thought of as Saxon, but both are older; going back to ancient Britain. Excavations in Kingston have revealed neolithic finds; coronation-stones were a Celtic custom before the Saxons. Cerdic who founded Alfred's line had a British name, a variant of Caradoc; his forbears Bron, Beldeg and Odin suspiciously resemble Bran, Belin and Gwydion - British god-kings to a man. Cerdic it seems was no pirate, landing at Southampton, but an emigre-scion of the old royal line, reclaiming his heritage. His family were the Gewissae, a name which might well be translated 'the wise.' Was this because they inherited Druid wisdom?

Merlin was also of the Gewissae, and no-one was wiser or more British than he. According to Arthurian Legend it was Merlin who made the original Round Table, which as

Katharine Maltwood has amply demonstrated, was the Glastonbury Zodiac, with Arthur, Guinevere and the chief knights seated about it as the twelve signs: the Grail-Quest being the search for these forgotten effigies in Avalon. (It was both an outer and inner quest, for the knights were also trying to find- *themselves*). Was this not the great secret passed from royal father to son, that Alfred inherited? ' There is a greater secret, known to few...the wand of Mathonwy on the bank of the river of spectres. Kynan shall obtain it when he comes to reign' - sang Taliesin the 6th century bard.

Merlin undoubtedly represented Druid tradition. But who taught Merlin? His tutor was one St. Bleise of Northumbria, Malory tells us in his ' Morte d' Arthur.' Is it accident merely, that Blaise appears in the centre of Kingston's Zodiac, painted in 1400 on the parish church's pillar?

Ostensibly this is St Blaise, patron saint of woolcombers and 3rd century bishop of Sebaste, who escaped Roman

SAINT BLAISE

persecution by escaping to the mountains, and befriending wild beasts. Here he learnt to speak with them. But hunters trapped him and took him back to Rome, where he was imprisoned and tortured for refusing to worship the emperor. They tore his flesh with iron combs, then threw him into the sea. But like the setting sun he walked on the water, thus converting many. He was at last beheaded, and this proved fatal! While in prison, an old woman whose pig he had saved by sweet-talking a wolf out of eating it, smuggled candles into his cell to light his Stygian darkness. His day, Feb.3rd, is Candlemas, when the winter sun is still weak. With his animals and his sunlike name it all sounds very like Zodiacal sun-myth baptised.

And oddly enough it was Candlemas when Merlin visited the other Bleise, his mentor. Arthur significantly enough had just won a battle with eleven kings - that is, with himself, the twelve Zodiac signs. (Morte d'Arthur, chap.15.) Merlin appeared before him disguised in wintry furs, and told him that on the site of that battle was a great treasure buried in the earth. Arthur strangely enough betrays no interest in this revelation, asks no questions, and the tale goes on to other matters. But we may well ask for him whether Merlin is not dropping a hint at the secret of the Zodiac? There are many others in Arthurian legend.

The common-sense reason for St Blaise in Kingston is that it has long been a market for sheep among other animals, so the wool-comb he holds could be useful. But Zodiac pilgrims may be forgiven for seeing its seven teeth as the seven rays of the sun, in view of his central position in its circle, his blazing name and his Candlemas connection with Arthurian legend.

Other old Kingston customs commemorate the Zodiacal seasons. 'Cracknut Sunday' when the congregation cracked nuts noisily throughout Michaelmas sermons, may have symbolised new life concealed within the dying husk of autumn. The King-game or Kingham was a maypole dance performed here for centuries by Robin on a hobbyhorse, with Maid Marion, Friar Tuck and assorted mummers - as an old print in the museum, now lost, used to show. Henry V111 sometimes attended incognito from Hampton Court - though how he disguised *his* figure is another question.. The maypole is the sun, its ribbons its multicoloured rays; perhaps also interweaving planetary influences. But Robin Hood and his merry men are much overlaid with sun-myth, like Arthur and his knights; Maid Marion echoes Guinevere, Friar Tuck Merlin, and lusty Little John Lancelot. While Robin shoots a last sunray at death into the forest, Bedivere hurls Arthur's sword Excalibur into the lake. Arthur is the hero of knightly Chivalry, while Robin became the people' s champion.

Kingston Museum has a Roman altar found in Eden Street and dedicated to the Goddess of Fortune. Who is she but Britannia with her Wheel? Did it recall the Zodiac wheel with Kingston at its centre? Odd, if not, that she should be worshipped here; for the Zodiac is indeed a Wheel of Fortune,

Kingston Market Place: as lively and busy today as in medieval times.

of seasons, birth, death and rebirth. It was these local clues and this Wessex history and sun-myth that made me undertake the task - daunting in such built-up areas - of trying to find the effigies.

Taking the hint from Kingston's 'Three Compasses' (now demolished) I drew a circle of five miles radius - the size of the Glastonbury Zodiac - from Kingston church. Westward it hit Sunbury's prehistoric boundary mound. The westering sun's setting-point? Sunbury Cross was also on it, where several ancient tracks meet. Hanworth Mound, also on an ancient cross-roads, was a near miss. Syon House, once a Brigittine monastery, was a northern point. It reminded me that St Brigit was carved on Glastonbury Tor's tower, a northern point in that Zodiac; and that Glastonbury has long been seen as Britain's Zion, New Jerusalem.. Brigit, a Celtic goddess whose name means ' bright', had nine Druidesses tending her perpetual fire, a custom the later St Brigit continued in her abbey at Kildare. She died about 525, but her nuns kept the sacred flames alight for centuries, until a pedantic Anglo-Norman overlord ordered them to be extinguished on the grounds that it was a pagan custom. But as soon as his back was turned they lit them again, to burn brightly for centuries more. There was a tower on Syon Hill in the Kingston Zodiac before the Gillette factory tower replaced it. Nine Gillette typists should tend a perpetual fire here to cheer travellers on the Great West Road.

Eastward the line passed between Putney and Fulham churches, which oppose each other across the Thames just as East and West Lydford churches flank the river Brue in the Somerset circle. Merton Priory and Nonsuch Palace (or rather, their sites, for both are now gone) were near my line, and so were Morden's and Claremont's mounds, and lastly, Walton-on-Thames, the Celts' or Waellas' town.

Such antiquities and coincidences were encouraging to further effort, but when the effigies began to appear, I soon found this circle too small. One of the most frequent objections to the existence of earth Zodiacs is 'But can't one make such figures on any map; especially in built-up areas, where there are so many roads to use?' All I can say is, I tried - and couldn't. Not on that scale, at least.

When Chessington's Lion first jumped out with a roar from old roads on the map, fortified by real lions at its Zoo (there are no lions anywhere else on this circle), I realised I was involuntarily following the Maltwood discovery - for Leo was the first figure she found. And when the two heads of the Gemini Twins appeared, clearly drawn by loops of the river Mole, just about where they should be - Gemini was her next find round Glastonbury - the sense of being part of a space-time pattern was overwhelming. The Thames and its tributaries seemed to govern the Kingston Zodiac, making it apparently a natural pattern. Once these two signs had given an indication of the scale, the other effigies appeared with varying degrees of difficulty; but the final circle was considerably larger than Glastonbury's; some 16 miles across. Very similar, it has the same changes from present-day Zodiacs; Libra and Aquarius being birds, its Cancer a boat, not a crab, while Sagittarius, like his Glastonbury counterpart, is a mounted archer, not a centaur. The Bull of the Kingston circle however is fully drawn, the ship a mere canoe, proportionately smaller.

The Guard Dog

The Cerberus of this circle rears his head near Egham; he stretches for seven miles to his tail.Though the Thames doesn't draw his back, it certainly governs the roads and paths that define it. Thorpe Park now graces his neck, and its large area has obscured the original paths that drew it. Holloway Sanatorium (recently made into luxurious flats) stands high and marks his nose for miles around. Our Dog has certainly suffered from modern development, for a railway now cuts off this nose. But does Prune Hill nearby remember his damp black muzzle?

I was told by someone who lived near neighbouring Callow Hill that Henry VIII's coffin burst open here as it rested here on its way to Windsor, and dogs licked his blood - fulfilling a prophecy made by a dispossessed monk. We shall find Dog stories abounding on this effigy. (The same grisly tale is told at Syon Park, on Capricorn's wintry grave.)

Lyne Lane obligingly lines his chest, while the parish boundary continues it down one foreleg to a paw at Longcross on Chobham Common, where there are barrows. Stonehill road draws the other foreleg to Stanners Hill and Foxhill. Were there standing stones here? There are certainly huge recumbent ones on the Army's training-grounds nearby.

Brooklands' once-famous race-track, now an aeroplane museum, draws a back leg. Dockett Point seems to indicate where the tail should be docked, but he nonetheless has a splendid one, its lower side recently helped by the cutting of Desborough Channel. Here was Dog Ait, another apt place-

RUNNYMEAD
EGHAM
THORPE
CHERTSEY
ADDLESTONE
OTTERSHAW
LALEHAM
LITTLETON
LITTLE DOG
SHEPPERTON

The Dog

name, where Charles I kept his hounds when hunting at neighbouring Oatlands. Zodiac pilgrims must regret that this clue has now gone, for it is now called Pharoah's Ait. There was once a Saxon village called Hundlesam here too, for good measure. Hamm is on his hams, where the river Wey draws them as it flows into the Thames. Just as well he is pent at Penton Hook on his collar, for this is no King Charles spaniel, but a champion of fiercer breed. (The Glastonbury Hound is also chained at Hook on his collar. I have already cited some of the many place-names that emphasise the fact that his effigy was once well-known.)

The Kingston Hound , like Glastonbury's, represents the constellation of Canis Major. Canis Minor, only drawn by his head, is just north of the Great Dog's tail at Littleton. A modern reservoir just misses him - luckily - for by strange coincidence Glastonbury's little dog, or just his head, is also at a place called Littleton.

But let us enter the Kingston Zodiac in style, through his eye at Great Fosters' noble Tudor pile, a hunting-lodge of Henry VIII near Egham. Oddly enough, "eghe" is the Saxon for eye. Perhaps it sparkles in the moat - or was it at Black Lake Farm next door? No-one here knows of a lake any more, however, when I enquired, lured by the magnificent half-timbered buildings of the farm. But these have all been reassembled from beams and bricks brought from demolished old barns elsewhere to create an impression of age - and remarkably well done. They are private dwellings; nothing remains of the original farm which must have supplied Henry's hunting-lodge.

Visit Great Fosters, now a hotel where you can obtain a meal in a stag-antlered hall worthy of Herne the Hunter himself, or just take a cup of tea beside the great fireplace. I remember seeing Cordoba leather wall-paper on the walls of one room, done for Anne Boleyn, but this has finally withered of old age.

Don't miss the serpent-tailed dogs carved over the porch, for Cerberus was often depicted thus; and note the superb ceilings and staircase. Wander in the Tudor gardens and don't be too surprised to find a spectacular sculptured Hound hiding behind the yew hedges! Not far off is his prey, a sculptured boar, reminding us that this place was once in Windsor forest. Nearby is an armillary sphere used by Henry Percy the astrologer-earl, one of two astrologers who suitably enough lived here. Imworth, the place was called in Saxon times; "imbre" meant a circle. Enter through the Dog's eye into this enchanted circle!

If the M25 is widened at this point it will be disastrous for Great Fosters, for it already passes at the end of the grounds. The M3 cuts through the Kingston Hound's jaw today, but concrete pillars carrying the M25 over it at this point have at least provided him with a fine new set of teeth - while the unceasing roar of traffic has given him a perpetual growl. Motorists, be warned. You are entering the Kingston Zodiac through the Dog's very jaws!

Take Herne for guide past Holloway Sanatorium's new flats to his nose across the railway, where the hollowest of hollow ways leads through an authentic remnant of Windsor Forest to Gorse Hill. It may be just gorse that named it, but I like to think that the Druids held Gorsedds here, at the entrance to this Zodiac.

The Dog's shoulder, raised on St Anne's Hill, is an old British camp defending the circle from the west. A beacon with fine views, its woodland paths and ramparts preserve a rural calm and beauty that make you quite forget the frenzied motorways below. World's End Lane here reinforces the message. Here the mundane world ends; the Otherworld begins.

Climbing this hill years ago in search of the Hound I was confronted with a picture of a black dog painted on a gatepost, with "Cave Canem" written beneath. On the hill-top was a gamekeeper's cottage with a summer-house on which an 18th. century tiled wall depicted armorial bearings supported by *two dogs*,one with red and white roses in their mouths. Sadly, these have since been vandalised and disappeared; so has the notice Cave Canem; but at the time I was greatly encouraged by them.

St Anne's Well is still here, from which the old defenders of this camp must have drunk. Who was she? Surely not the ghostly nun who still haunts this hill and was walled up here for trysting with a lover? No, she must once have been the old witch Black Annis, still worshipped until recently in remote parts of the British Isles, who named so many hills before St Anne baptised them. Virgo of the Glastonbury Zodiac has an Annis Hill, and Irish mountains, the Paps of Anu remember her. Our ancestors (like Henry Moore) saw all rounded hills as the Mother Goddess's breasts, the streams flowing from them her " Liebfraumilch" which nourished her children. But

unlike the Christian Virgin she had a dark aspect, for her wild sons Gwyn and Gwythyr with their howling wish-hounds put the wind up the Celts, hunting dying souls on stormy nights for their Underworld. They probably put the wind in Windsor and Windlesham too, for Gwyn was not only the Lord of Glastonbury Tor, but is probably one with Herne the Hunter of Windsor Forest. His hounds can still sometimes be heard baying on wild winter nights, as letters to the local papers attest.

Gwyn and Gwythyr appear in the Welsh Mabinogion; if the G in Gwythyr's name is aspirated in the Welsh manner he equates with Arthur and his father Uther. And the Arthur of folklore also swept over the hills with a pack of roaring wish-hounds on stormy nights. "Arthur MacArthur, the big-bellied ben - He goes roaring down the glen" as an old Scots nursery rhyme put it. It is notable too that Mistress Quickly when mourning the death of Falstaff, sighs "A's gone to Arthur's bosom." Not Abraham's bosom, the more usual phrase, but *Arthur's.* Plainly in Shakespeare's day Arthur was not seen just as a historical character by the peasantry, but someone more godlike.

Herne, who as we shall see acquired antlers, is also identified with the horned forest-god Cernunnos who appears on several Celtic carvings and on the famous Gundestrup bowl surrounded by wild woodland creatures. As Herne's tale is local and involves hunting dogs, it belongs here. He was Richard II's favourite huntsman, and saved his master's life by interposing his body between the king and a charging stag, but was mortally wounded. However, a mysterious stranger appeared, and binding the stag's horns on Herne's brow, promised to heal him in his hut at Bagshot, in the deepest part of Windsor forest.

But the other huntsmen were jealous of the chief hunstsman's skill and royal favour, and threatened to kill the stranger if

Herne recovered. Compromising, he cured him, but bereft him of his hunting skill. This soon became apparent when he returned to his work, and the ungrateful Richard finding him hopelessly incompetent angrily dismissed him. The hunter in despair hanged himself on what was long known as Herne's oak. His dying curse drew the huntsmen to the spot, and his horned ghost appeared, leading them against their will on a wild midnight hunt; nor could they stop until all the king's deer were exterminated. Needless to say, Richard had them all hanged. And struck with remorse and fear for his hunting, he repaired to Herne's oak and invoked the ghostly hunter, imploring his forgiveness and begging him to revenge himself no more. Herne, appeased, magically returned the deer to life, promising not to indulge in such an orgy again - at least while Richard lived.

It is a curious fact of history that Richard, whose symbol was the White Hart, did not live long, being himself rent by Bolingbroke who, soured by unjust banishment, returned to usurp the throne as Henry IV, while Richard died mysteriously in prison. But though Henry and his son Henry V strongly kept the throne, the pack had tasted blood; and the succession once troubled brought on the Wars of the Roses. A strange parallel. Barons should keep the realm for the benefit of all, not devour it; just as huntsmen should preserve the forest and its deer. Mayhem ensues when the guard-dogs turn poachers.

Something of Cernunnos' (or Herne's) rites may survive in the old antlered dance of Abbot's Bromley. These antlers, annually renewed, were perhaps a symbol of seasonal and spiritual death and rebirth. In fact some have seen Cernunnos as a god who underwent a transformation mystery. Beside him on the great Gundestrup Bowl human figures (doubtless initiates in his mysteries) are being tipped into a cooking pot which must be Ceredwen's cauldron of inspiration, transformation and rebirth. Was Cernunnos the son of

Ceredwen, or Kerin the Nun, as his name seems to hint? Into her earthy cauldron all things are consigned at death, and emerge renewed.

Herne, alias Cernunnos, is the Green Man, Lord of Nature; an ecological figure, who demands justice for the green earth. Maltreat him and he decimates the forest's wild life. Shakespeare's Merry Wives of Windsor believed that if angered he blighted trees and soured the milk. .Ignore his ecology and he pollutes our food and drink; feed his vegetarian cows and sheep with carnivorous offal, drench them in organo-phosphates, and they go mad... His story hints that he balances social forces too; neglect him and we court revolution or civil war. He demands compassion and justice for all living creatures, and a bonus - or bone - for his dog - a sop to Cerberus, for good measure..
Another local legend with a canine flavour also has to do with King and barons in conflict. It was said round here that King John, forced to sign Magna Carta at Runnymede, was so enraged he turned into a wolf! And Perry Oaks, now lying under Heathrow's runways nearby, claimed to be the village where the last wolf in England was killed.

Chertsey still dreams of the Wars of the Roses. The vanished dogs on St Anne's Hill held a rose in their mouths, and the town's famous legend is set at that time. Needless to say, it also features a hound, so must be told.

The May-Queen Blanche Heriot of Chertsey hid her Lancastrian lover Neville Audley from his Yorkist pursuers in an upstairs cupboard in her father's house, but their bloodhound smelt him out, and in desperation he took it by the throat and strangled it, throwing it downstairs. (So Hercules strangled Cerberus, throwing him down into Hades). But Neville was caught nevertheless and condemned to die at curfew. Blanche sent an urgent messenger to London to obtain the king's pardon, but as the hour of curfew drew near and the pardon delayed, this heroine of the poem "Curfew shall not ring tonight" ran up the church tower as the bell was about to strike and hung on its clapper with her bare hands, muffling the sound and swinging with it until it ceased, and the royal pardon came clattering over Chertsey Bridge. Neville strangled the belling hound; Blanche, bruised and bleeding, strangled the bell. Together they cheated death, its hell-hound and its knell.

There are strange coincidences here. Chertsey Abbey was founded on the Hound's back in AD 666 - the Number of the Beast. Blanche Heriot's name recalls the mediaeval "heriot beast" - an animal that was loaned by the squire to his tenant and had to be returned on the tenant's death. How much of this tale is history - and how much is myth? The name Heriot seems as if it were chosen for its association with beasts. And can Chertsey's Curfew, one of few still rung today, secretly remember that a watchdog was once called a *Cur*? A delightful statue of Blanche desperately hanging on the bell now stands near Chertsey Bridge, so this enigmatic tale will not be forgotten.

Alas, not much remains now of this once-splendid abbey, but enough for a visit. A few stones, a barn, a gateway, are all there is now to remind us. But to X-ray eyes it can still vibrate transparently against the trees, rising from humble Saxon arches to cascades of Gothic tracery, and sinking again like a ghostly fountain into the mists of time...

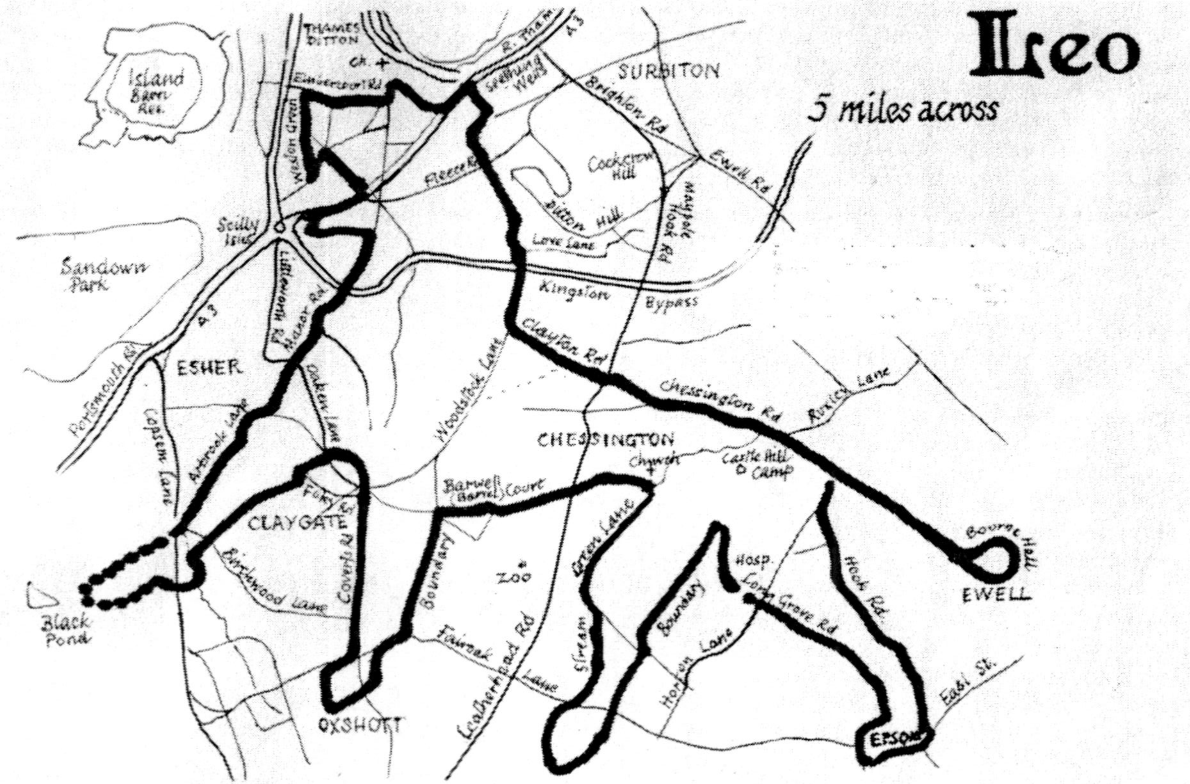
Leo
5 miles across
Island Barn Res.
THAMES DITTON
Ch.
Embercourt Rd
Weston Green
R. Thames
A3
Stevens Wood
SURBITON
Brighton Rd
Ewell Rd
Cockcrow Hill
Ditton Hill
Maypole
Hook Rd
Love Lane
Fleece Rd
Scilly Isles
Sandown Park
Littleworth Rd
Manor Rd
Kingston Bypass
Clayton Rd
Portsmouth Rd
ESHER
Oaken Lane
Woodstock Lane
Chessington Rd
Rushett Lane
Copsem Lane
Arbrook Lane
CHESSINGTON
Church
Castle Hill Camp
Barwell (Barrel) Court
Foley Rd
CLAYGATE
Coverts Rd
Birchwood Lane
Black Pond
Boundary
Zoo
Green Lane
Hosp.
Long Grove Rd
Hook Rd
Bourne Hall
EWELL
Fairoak Lane
Leatherhead Rd
Stream
Horton Lane
OXSHOTT
East St.
EPSOM

Leo

Let us enter the circle with Leo, as he was the first figure Katharine Maltwood found - and the first one I found too, by strange coincidence. Leo is ruled by the sun, and the sun-god par excellence is Hercules. He is not just the muscle-bound hero of Greek myth; his twelve Labours were his struggles as an initiate in the Mysteries to analyse and come to terms with the different Zodiac aspects of his own character. As his first Labour was an encounter with the Nemean Lion, there is classical precedence for beginning here. And perhaps to find Leo first is no accident, but an indication that those who search for such effigies are entering the Mysteries, whether they are aware of it or not.

Leo has two possible heads, one on Surbiton's Cockcrow Hill, the other, more resplendent, at Thames Ditton. (The Mysteries in suburbia? Where else, since most of us live now in such districts.) Leo can startle you with a roar when trains thunder overhead as you enter the railway tunnel on his open jaws on the Portsmouth Road, to remind you that everyday life has more overtones than you are aware of. The old road from Chessington to Ewell draws his back and tail, its tuft at rounded Bourne Hall. His belly or barrel is Barwell Lane. Spelt Burrel on Rocque's old map it must have been pronounced like barrel - and meant it.

Leo ruled by the sun is a royal sign, and palaces surround him - Hampton Court is just across the Thames from his head, Nonsuch Palace was just east of his tail at Nonsuch. The reason he was comparatively easy to see on the map is that much of his figure was long kept open as royal hunting-grounds from these palaces. Being Crown land it has avoided being built over, and since been preserved as part of London's Green Belt. So only Claremont, built more recently by Clive of India, is actually on his effigy. But it too became royal, being home to the youthful Queen Victoria, who later gave it to the exiled French king Louis-Philippe whose family occupied it for some generations. *No less than three royal Leopolds, aptly named*, lived here, one after the other.

All three palaces are scenes of royal love-matches - and bitter sorrow - Leo's path to wisdom. Leo in astrology has many loves but few children; Henry VIIIs thwarted struggles for an heir are typical. Leopold, Victoria's uncle and later king of the Belgians, lost his beloved wife Charlotte in childbirth after only one year of marriage; in Claremont's day of mourning England lost two heirs to the throne at one fell swoop, for Charlotte was George IV's daughter, due to succeed him. Charles II, also famous for his many loves, had no legitimate children. He made Epsom on Leo's hind foot famous; racing is the sport of kings.

Real Lions roar on Leo at Chessington World of Adventures - and nowhere else on this Zodiac. What an extraordinary coincidence! It was the first of several I encountered in my search, and one that shook my initial scepticism. It is on the Leatherhead road, and this town's quaint name was once Leret, Ledridan, even *Leo*driden. Was Leatherhead named from the old road - the high and dry way through Leo? It is certainly ancient,. Druids Grove lies beside it south of Leatherhead., and it leads past a barrow on Surbiton's Cock-Crow hill down to romantically named Seething Wells on the Thames. If these artesian springs, visited by rheumatic Britons as a spa, still have the power to seethe they have long been sadly invisible, having been piped by the Water Board. Thames Water is sitting on them now, like a toad at the mouth of the well, and doesn't want to know. What a splendid day it would be for Kingston if they were allowed to seethe again!

Chessington's Winey Hill is said to get its name from Roman vineyards, and Green Lane was a Roman road running from the old church to a Roman villa in Ashtead woods. But even earlier Britons of some substance lived in Chessington, for a hoard of gold coins (Leo's metal!) of 150 BC have been found here; they are now in Kingston Museum.

Chessington's World of Adventures reminds us that Leo's 5th House is concerned with leisure, pleasure - and children. Here are not only live lions, but a whole Zodiac of animals. Stone lions moreover are everywhere in the grounds; the heraldic device - aptly enough - of the family who lived in the old manor. It was called Burnt Stubs because it was burnt in the Civil War. Leo is a fire-sign!

Is it accident merely that Enid Blyton who has delighted so many children , wrote her tales at Hook, on Leo's mane? It was his countryside (more rural in her day than it is now) round here that fired her imagination. Surbiton's coat of arms has a lion too. Its St Mark's church is well-named, for St Mark, one of the four evangelists, has always been signed by a lion. (The four signs taken by early Christians to symbolise the evangelists were originally the four fixed signs of the Zodiac, the Bull, Lion, Eagle and Man.)

Charming old Thames Ditton on Leo's head has not only a Red Lion Inn, but a Lion House in its High Street, with Leo House nearby on the Portsmouth Road. Lord St Leonard owned Boyle Farm by the church, and much land round here- which accounts for St Leonard's Road. What he didn't own belonged to the Lovelace family, equally well-named as Leo is Lord of Love; several Surbiton roads are named after them.

The church has a Norman tower and font (Surrey's best) and with its Tudor brasses of Hampton Courtiers and countrified air is well worth a visit. To its credit, it still keeps open., at least at the time I write. An Arian Paschal Lamb, a Star of

Thames Ditton Church.

David and an enigmatic goat upside down are carved on the font. These symbols are characteristic of the Templars. Perhaps they were once at Hampton Court, for excavations there have revealed foundations of a hostelry of the Knights of St John, who inherited much Templar property after that Order was suppressed. Gibbon derided the Templars for "being led by a goat and a goose." (You can drink to this goose in Thames Ditton's delightful old Swan Inn, looking out over the Thames.)

But why is the goat upside-down? Some say he is the goat-god Nicor who was worshipped at fords in pagan times, and as the church is on the Thames with an island at this point, there could well have been a summer ford-crossing here over to Hampton Court, when the river was low. Nicor,perhaps upside-down to reverse his pagan power, has since been christened St. Nicholas. But Nicholas himself is Santa Claus - a mid-winter saint, and Capricorn the goat begins the winter solstice upside-down on the Zodiac; so researchers like myself may be forgiven for seeing this figure as a reminder of the polarity of the Lion of Summer and the topsy-turvy Capricorn of winter.

The connection that links the goat-god with fords seems to be solstitial Capricorn, when the sun is at its weakest hour, seems to die and is due to be renewed. Ageing Celtic sun-gods often battled with their up-coming rivals at fords, or water's edge, the loser sinking beneath the waves. Capricorn is sometimes shown emerging from a shell, indicating that he rises from a watery grave. In the brief absence of the sun, Lord of Heaven, chaos reigns. Then the Yuletide Lord of Misrule, horned and cleft-footed, could stamp out his antic dance. The Catholic Church rightly suspects Santa Claus of pagan origins. But long may he cheer the shortest nights, despite papal frowns!

FITZGERALD
LADY EDWARD FITZGERALD'S
REMAINS WERE REMOVED FROM PARIS BY
J.P LEONARD ESQ AND INTERRED HERE THE
27th AUGUST 1880 BY HER GRANDCHILDREN
THE ABOVE STONE WAS ON HER TOMB
IN MONTMARTRE CEMETERY AND WAS
BROKEN BY THE BURSTING OF A SHELL
DURING THE SIEGE OF 1870.

Capricorn's horn, long and single, suggests the Unicorn, and Lion and Unicorn were connected in mediaeval minds, well before they appeared as supporters of our royal coat of arms. For they symbolised not only summer and winter, but the polarity of Leo, the dominant power of Church or State, versus Capricorn, the elusive Unicorn or White Hart of secret wisdom-teachings, whose survival often depended on camouflage or flight. When the Lion beat the Unicorn all round the town, Druids, the Celtic Church, Gnostics, Cathars, Templars, Rosicrucians were suppressed, and dominant Leo became a tyrant.

The Grand Master of the Templars, burning in Paris after long torture, uttered a dying curse. Yet it was more a prophecy than a curse, predicting the social consequences when the balance of Lion and Unicorn is destroyed. Witch and heretic burnings became endemic, massacres and religious wars, plague and famine ensued for centuries. Nine generations of French kings died by violence, so that even the victorious Lion suffered. Yet still the White Hart survives in the depths of the forest, to be sought by every prince of folklore.....

In St Nicholas churchyard is a romantic grave, that of tragic Lady Pamela Fitzgerald, a famous but ill-fated beauty of the French Revolution. Hers is a truly royal Leonine tale of tyranny, love and love-loss, which you can read in several biographies in Thames Ditton Library. She was said to be the illegitimate daughter of the Duke of Orleans and his countess-mistress Madame de Genlis, who was also his childrens' governess..Fearing for her reputation, she smuggled her babe to England. One can understand her dilemma, for she had published moralistic books on child-education. But she missed her daughter sorely, and after four years hit upon a brilliant plan to bring her back. Giving out that they needed a little girl from Britain to teach the Duke's children English, they "found" her and " adopted" her, her without acknowledging her true origin. As she grew up in their court her beauty became famous, and when the Revolution came she was tempestuously wooed and won by handsome young Lord Edward Fitzgerald , who saved her from the guillotine that was to kill her father, and whisked her to Boyle Farm, Thames Ditton, where Edward's brother lived.

But Edward had become MP for Athy in Ireland, and it was not long before his compassionate heart, shocked at the desolate state in which he found the indigenous Irish, spoke out fierily in Dublin's parliament on their behalf. But finding stiff resistance to any reforms, he lost patience, and secretly joined the seditious Irish Nationalists under Wolfe Tone. By now he and Pamela had three young children, but he had to leave them and go underground. Planning a liberating invasion of Ireland by the French, a price was put on his head and it was not long before he was betrayed, apprehended in Dublin and shot, resisting arrest. In a month he die in prison of his wounds, leaving her with her young children and no means of support, for his possessions were confiscated. Widow of a man who to the Irish was a shining martyr, but to the English a traitor, Pamela had to leave England and wandered about Europe for many years, penniless and relying on the generosity of friends, and was forced to leave her children with her husband's family in Thames Ditton. Even her French Countess-mother who had somehow survived the guillotine and could have helped, repudiated her, determined to the end to deny that Pamela was her daughter; and she died at the age of 59 in Paris, the subject of envious scandal, quite undeserved, to the last. It was an ardent admirer of Lord Edward who brought her body back to Thames Ditton, where she now lies among her children and grand-children, from whom she was in life so long parted.

The Maypole Inn at Hook must long have been the scene of Leo's rustic summer rave-ups. Does the word Hook come from "hoch!" ejaculated by Scottish dancers to make them leap higher? The swords of passion held aloft and woven into a star are a sublimation symbol, as Hook's North Star Inn reminds us. Somerset's Leo also has Maypole Knap on his effigy. Or is Hook there to tether Leo? In Arthurian legend the lion was chained to a rock, again signifying emotional energy, harnessed and sublimated in the Mysteries.

Leo is the Lord of Love., and Love Lane, still green, is on his mane at Hook. From here lovers can walk intertwined in leisure hours down Woodstock Lane into Oxshott Woods, Chessington's rolling pastures, or Claygate and Epsom's Commons.. But let them beware of the Surrey Leopard, who though he has not been seen lately, was said to roam these glades... Was he the ghost of Leo? Perhaps they should mark Lord Foley's Folly too, towering aloft to warn them that Leo's amorous follies can destroy, like the lion unchained. Much they care! Live now, pay later - make hay while the sun shines - a short life and a merry one - all these are Leo's mottos.

It is the suffering of love loss, more than any other problem, that is the Gate to the Mysteries - that drives us in despair to seek some point and purpose in our lives. Some who cannot

find this gate to meaning and hope collapse into asylums. Several of these cluster on Leo's hindquarters at Horton - aptly - for mental disorder is usually emotional at base. Leo shines like the sun when he is loved; he is at his best surrounded by a circle of admirers to whom he can give of his generous nature. Deprive him of these and he is a sorry lion. But let him take courage and remember that such loss, far from being meaningless, is an invitation to another octave; it is designed as a gate to higher meaning and understanding. "Man, Know Thyself" is written over this Gate of Sorrows.

Visit Chessington's ancient church, built on an even older mound. An 18th.century west window shows four lions' heads, like compass-points to give your bearings. Leo lies all around you; Green Lane, still invitingly green, runs down one hind leg, the other takes you to Epsom. Nearby is Castle Hill, site of a farm said to be Saxon, though Roman coins have been anachronistically found there; westward is Winey Hill which contours a front leg and has lovely views. The church (St Mary's) seems set to hallow love, being on Leo's most potent part.

So don't miss the mediaeval marble of the Annunciation set in the chancel wall, which indeed hallows love. A dove (surely Leo's sun-ray) plummets toward the Virgin (Virgin-soil, the Earth-Mother) to inseminate her with new life, while lilies (or the fleur-de-lys) spring up from the ground in response. This theme is older than Christianity, though adopted by it - for many earlier sun-gods descended to earth in bird-form to fertilise earth-maidens. The theme belongs to earlier Mysteries; the dove, lilies and the Druids' broad arrow of inspiration all express the same idea.

Virgo

Chaste Virgo has chased Leo to Chase End, Epsom. Obviously she has not always been so chaste as she seemed in Chessington Church..But he resolutely turns his back, trying to ignore her effrontery in wearing his tufted tail on her bonnet in the the middle of Ewell High Street. She must be the first tuft-hunter of all! (Note Chase End and Headway here on the A to Z.)

She has many names all over the country, this White Goddess, being the timeless triple goddess of all myth. . As the only female of the Zodiac she must be all women in one - at once spring maiden, fruitful mother of summer and screaming hag of winter. And many names on her effigy here hint at this. As White Eve (Guinevere) of Epsom and Ewell - (Eve's or Ebba's Ham and well) she is young, seductive; as Ban the Banshee she is the bane of Bandon Hill, Benhill and Banstead. Bhan is old Gaelic for woman, and Banon Welsh for Queen. (Yet it must be remembered that Bun the Maid of the Welsh Mabinogion is the same name, and she can give us boons - and even buns - when we need them. There are various legends of merciful ladies who subjected themselves to humiliation to persuade their mean lords and masters to give land or bread to the poor, like Lady Godiva - God-Eva - who must be one with the lady of *Banbury* on her white horse.) Was there a coven at Coventry where she was worshipped?

Suburban Cheam, once Ceiham, may remember her as the British Ceres - Ceredwen, or Ched the witch of Cheddar cave and Wookey Hole, who has given us cheese as well as buns - for Chadacre Road, doubtless an old field-name, is near her face at Nonsuch. At Carshalton she is Mother Carey. Such was her prestige that Christians, wisely deciding that if you

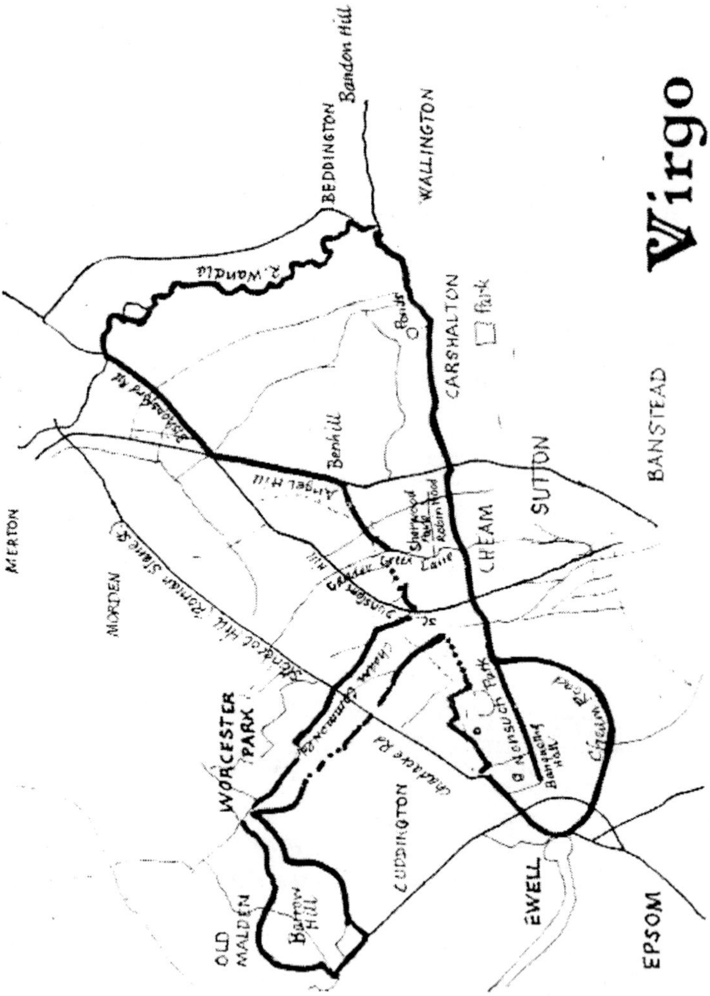
MERTON
MORDEN
WORCESTER PARK
OLD MALDEN
Barrow Hill
CUDDINGTON
EWELL
EPSOM
BANSTEAD
SUTTON
CHEAM
CARSHALTON
WALLINGTON
BEDDINGTON
Bandon Hill
R. Wandle
Benhill
Angel Hill
Nonsuch Park
Cheam Rd
Park
Ponds

Virgo

can't beat 'em, join 'em, built a magnificent priory to her at Merton. (It's true that Merton is really into Scorpio, but Virgo's benign influence seems to extend into the death-sign, as we shall see when we enter Scorpio.) A monastery nestled in her hair at Ewell, and St Dunstan, harping his way from priory to friary, erected a chapel on her breast (now called the Lumley Chapel) at Cheam.

There are some delightful old buildings here, showing Cheam as more ancient than it looks at first glance. Visit lovely Whitehall, where you can have coffee and be shown around its hoary beams. As Maid Marion her heart is pierced by the Archer's arrow at Sutton's Sherwood Park and Robin Hood Lane - via the bird of Gander Green Lane. They say that Merton church (St. Mary's) was founded by a Saxon who saw the site suddenly illumined by a heavenly shaft of light. The arrow-bird's descent Virgin-wards?

We must be grateful to Henry VIII, that famous decapitator of queens, for preserving Virgo's head in Nonsuch Park. You can see her face clearly on the map at the park gates - her nose a triangular copse, her profile drawn by a ditch, now dry; her eye a willow-fringed pond, just where it should be. You may address your prayers to her right in her ear, a deeply sunk amphitheatre convoluted by rhododendron beds. Or if prayer is not your thing, try wishing... And as she is Martha as well as Mary, she will refresh you here with tea and ice-cream in the summer months.

She might have posed for Tenniel as the Red Queen in *Alice;* she is also surely the first seated Britannia, her Trident (or wheatsheaf) rounded by Barrow Hill, Old Malden. Her seated figure is remarkably like her constellation in the sky. No sex-kitten, this severe Queen of Heaven; she is Boadicea, Elizabeth, Florence Nightingale, Victoria, all rolled into one - a very English type. No wonder Englishmen fled in despair and created the Empire. Yet the name Nonsuch suits this

Virgin non-pareille, and she was adored from a respectful distance.

Diana's Ditch on her head equates her with the Virgin huntress; fleet Diana like the Red Queen commands men to run faster, faster, if they would keep pace with evolution. No feather-bed-mates, these Amazons; was it at Nonsuch that Queen Elizabeth kicked the Spanish ambassadors teeth in when he knelt at her feet?

For she was often here, and you can see exactly where the palace was; it was found after extensive excavations and covered over again, after marking the site with memorial pillars. The foundation walls of Queen Elizabeth's Banqueting Hall are still there, beside the Ewell bypass. We can imagine the grand scenes, the farthingales, the velvet cloaks and plumed hats of the nobles and their ladies, as they rode on caparisoned horses to the feasts, drawn not only from English shires but from all Europe to this peerless palace, built over poor Cuddington's cruelly demolished village, expressly to overawe the high and mighty. (Does Cuddington's name not also derive from Ced?)

There is a certain irony and justice in that we, the plebs, can now walk over this peaceful greensward at will. Perhaps while there we should imagine not only the kings and queens, lords and ladies whose ghosts flit unseen past us - even through us - but give a thought to the distraught villagers of Cuddington, fleeing in all directions while their humble dwellings were burnt or pulled down about their ears by Henry's uncaring command; their allotment vegetables, all that sustained them, given over to his royal deer to eat. His Great Park once stretched north to Worcester Park, so named because the Earl of Worcester, at one time its Keeper, had a large mansion there.

The strange coincidence that Roman Stane Street which runs from London Bridge to Chichester, passes down Virgo's front just as the ancient Fosse Way from Exeter to Lincoln does to her Somerset sister, has already been mentioned. One wonders what the significance of this can have. Whatever it was, it was noted by the Norman-French History of the Holy Grail (which so accurately describes the Glastonbury effigies) naming Virgo as "the Damsel beyond the Bar."

Boadicea , a very formidable Virgoan figure, battled her way against the Romans down Stane Street, some say to final defeat at Mickleham. Did she make a stand on Virgo's bonnet, where the foundations of Queen Elizabeth's banqueting Hall still remain? A huge raised causeway defines the back of her head; was this the original Ewell Castle, older by far than the Victorian battlemented school of that name in the valley below ?

Linger in Ewell's watery charm; its mills, old manors and a ruined church tower will lead you down the corridors of time. Its Victorian church replacing the mediaeval one is dedicated to the Virgin. Its springs are the source of the Hogsmill river which attracted those PreRaphaelite artists Millais and Holman Hunt so much that they painted at least four pictures on its banks. As young men in 1851 they spent a whole day wandering along it in search of suitable backgrounds for the paintings they had in mind. (Holman Hunt had often stayed with his aunt and uncle in the farm next the church, so he knew Ewell well, and Millais had friends who also lived there.)

It has always been thought that Millais' background for his famous picture of Ophelia drowning was the river in Ewell. But a careful researcher, Barbara Webb, who knows the district well, read their voluminous letters written at the time, and has discovered the exact spot where Millais "drowned" Ophelia. She has written a booklet describing how to get there. Those who want to see where its background was painted should follow a rural path downhill from Old Malden church, cross the river by a footbridge, and turn left along its bank for a few yards into 6-Acre Meadow. Here, looking across the stream, is a rising bank, just as in the painting; with the same dog-roses and the same willow, still growing there. Ophelia - what a Virgoan subject! And the site is on Virgo's Wheatsheaf. Virgo is meticulous, and loves detail, and truth to detail was one of the PreRaphaelites' aims; they took immense care to paint each plant, flower and leaf so that they were immediately recognisable.

But it was only the background for Ophelia that Millais painted there; the story of how he put his model Elizabeth Siddall in a bath in his studio, is well-known. It was lit below by a lamp to keep her and the water warm, but he painted so enthusiastically he forgot to refuel the lamp; it went out, and his freezing model caught a bad chill. Her enraged father wanted to sue the young painter, but was eventually persuaded to settle the matter out of court.

While Millais worked at Old Malden, Holman Hunt painted his "Hireling Shepherd" in a field near Ewell Court Farm. They stayed at this time at the original Nonsuch Park-Keeper's house, which had by then become Worcester Park Farm. Millais also painted " The Huguenot" on the banks of the Hogsmill.

It was not until about two years later that Holman Hunt painted his famous " Light of the World" - of Christ holding a *glowing lamp*, knocking at a long-unused door overgrown with weeds. It has always been assumed that this was Old Malden's church door, but the indefatigable Barbara Webb has found from his memoirs that this was the long-locked door of a hut that once belonged to the gunpowder mills that he had found on a night walk along the Hogsmill river, *very near the scene of Ophelia's drowning.*The choice of a powdermill door may have suggested to him that nothing less than an explosion would open it. .

Church doors in his day were well-oiled and well-used - quite unsuitable for Hunt's proposed theme of Christ knocking at the door of our hardened hearts with no response. Was the idea prompted at this spot by a memory of poor Elizabeth Siddall's extinguished lamp - a tale he must often have heard from his friend Millais? And did Virgo herself stimulate his unconscious at this moment to remember Christ's parable of the Foolish Virgins, whose lamps were empty when the Bridegroom appeared, so that they were shut out from the wedding feast? The time, the place, and Christ's glowing lamp, all help to make one wonder.

Old Malden with its picturesque Plough Inn and secret cell that hid Dick Turpin; its still-surviving duck-pond, its church with Saxon foundations and the views from steep Barrow Hill, is even today an oasis in suburbia. Norman Walter de Merton founded a school under Barrow Hill. (Many of our oldest schools were founded on or beneath such ancient mounds or hills - perhaps a surviving custom from Druidic Gorsedd-mounds. Read E.O.Gordon's *Prehistoric London* on this subject.) Was Walter influenced, consciously or unconsciously, by studious Virgo's love of learning?

Zodiacs seem to attend him wherever he went. He was an abbot of Merton Priory, and Merton College, Oxford's oldest college, which he also founded, has a mediaeval Zodiac. There is another at Rochester Cathedral, where he later became bishop..If you doubt that this Victorian example is revived from an early one, look at the mediaeval painting of the Wheel of Fate on the wall of the cathedral, or study its west door with its Norman (and Zodiacal) evangelists' beasts. Canterbury Cathedral has a mediaeval Zodiac - why not Rochester too?

Walter's passion for education was like Alfred's. He wished that learning should not be confined to the church, but become general. In an age when it was jealously guarded within monastery walls, he stipulated that scholars of Merton College should not join a closed order but spread their enthusiasm among the laity.

The Merton College Zodiac follows the earth-Zodiac pattern in making its goat fourfooted, not a goat-fish; sculptured in stone, it hangs like ripe grapes from the college gateway's ceiling, symbolising its founder's liberality. (Walter may have been liberal in more ways than one; was the dear bishop quite sober when he fell in the Medway and drowned?)

Our Virgin stretches from Ewell to Beddington; though much of her effigy is now suburban, the character of the houses and streets is generally modest, neat and somewhat prim like hers; nothing too small nor too big; nothing too ostentatious. All lawns are meticulously mown, all bills paid on time. In fact it is notable that the characters of all the signs are reflected in their areas - as we shall see. The Zodiac's 6th. House of Health is Virgo' s, and she tends to be something of a hypochondriac - so it is not surprising to find at least three well-known hospitals on her effigy.

The Virgin-Queen Elizabeth often rode the length of this sign from Nonsuch to see her Celtic friends the Cornish and Welsh Carews at Beddington Manor. The keeper of Carshalton Park assured me that her horse kicked a stone here and thus started the Wandle river flowing. It has indeed a source in this park, though one imagines it has been flowing longer than that. But reflecting that all Virgin Queens are essentially one, I saw what he meant, and was grateful for the legend... Here are intriguing mounds, a strange rectangular pit called the Hogspond, and a huge ancient elm stump to heighten the mystery. Carshalton's Mother Carey smiles enigmatically behind her prim exterior. What's with these elms of Virgo's? Another monstrous stump is on her hand at Worcester Park's dairy farm, emulating her wheatsheaf; yet another, "Queen Elizabeth's Elm," is marked on Nonsuch Park maps near Diana's Ditch. (On the Somerset Virgin's skirt at Foddington was a huge elm stump that could accommodate two farm carts; whole families used to picnic in it before it was destroyed.)

Ann Boleyn, Elizabeth's mother, is remembered at Carshalton's beautiful Ponds. Her statue and well are there, and a pensioner with whom I shared a bench confided that she used to bathe her feet in these ponds. On the hem of Virgo's skirt! I thought inwardly. But alas for experts. They doubt now that she was ever there, and that her legend has grown from the local manorial family name of Boulogne, which could easily be corrupted over time into Boleyn.Long may her statue remain, notwithstanding. For Anne not only in myth and art, but in history, is the dark mother of the Virgin. Shades of Black Annis! Ann Boleyn was thought a witch because she had webbed fingers, or so some say. She certainly bewitched Henry VIII.

And Virgo can undoubtedly be bewitching. Count the chorus of beauties who have graced (and sometimes disgraced) her here - from Kenwhal's fatal Fair Maid of Merton to Nelson's. Lady Hamilton lived at Carshalton and later at Merton. Jenny Lind lived at Sutton. Henry's last queens and Charles II's many loves all played kiss-in-the-ring at Nonsuch. Charles II, infatuated with the duchess of Kerouaille, (Squintabella, as her envious rivals unkindly called her) paid off his discarded mistress Barbara Villiers by giving her Nonsuch Palace. But Barbara, Duchess of Cleveland, was an inveterate gambler, and soon sold it to the knackers to pay her debts. So the stones of doomed Nonsuch, which had largely come from ruined Merton Priory, went poetically enough still further down the Stane street to build the first grandstand for Epsom racecourse.

Nor must we forget among Virgo's beauties the Fair Maid of Kent, Richard II's mother, who owned Tolworth Court Farm on Virgo's wheatsheaf beside the Hogsmill river,- and sent her son to school at Kingston. (The last decaying barn of this mediaeval farm only fell down finally a few years ago; many on the road from Kingston to Ewell must have watched its slow decline with regret as they passed it on the corner of Worcester Park Road. But at least local archaeologists have excavated on the site and recorded their finds.)

Is it not poetic that the roads defining Virgo's skirt should be called Rose Hill and Angel Hill? Poetic too the Three Kings pub that stands on its hem at Mitcham. Though some say it really remembers the Saxon kings who died fighting the Danes on the Wandle river, it is for Zodiac pilgrims as if the Three Kings from the Orient had come to worship at the Virgin's feet.

Wallington nearby, Wales Farm Road, Acton, on Capricorn's hind foot, and Walton on Thames on Taurus the Bull's, are three tell-tale place-names that bound this Zodiac. They all mean Welsh-town; and could be seen as gates to this long-obscured sacred circle of the Waellas. St Dunstan the Glastonbury bishop and alchemist, here rememberd by St Dunstan's Hill, built chapels on various places on its perimeter - the one at Cheam already mentioned, a friary on Capricorn's hind foot at Wales Farm Road known as St Dunstan's Bakery; and two churches at Feltham on Taurus' tail-tuft and Piscean Cranford. Those of sounder (or more conventional) mind must forgive Zodiac enthusiasts for seeing this as further confirmation that he knew of the circle.

The Cornish and Welsh Carews built their splendid Surrey seat in the 1300s at Beddington near Carshalton. As branches of this notable family were also called Cary in times when spelling was vague, this seems an odd coincidence. Did they know where they were and build their mansion at the

Kingston Virgin's feet, in homage to their west-country ancestral goddess Mother Cary, all drawn by the river Cary in Avalon's Zodiac? Since the Carews have departed after several centuries of occupation, this Mother-Goddess, who cares for all, has made it into a Special School - so that many with no other hope will benefit and develop in this magnificent setting.

Beddington with its extensive Park is still beautiful, still mysterious with its ghostly grey lady who sometimes rises from the misty Wandle river. Beddington's Celtic name means "place of graves", and there were barrows here, testifying to its ancient sanctity. Its church has an old Roman sarcophagus, a Norman font, and has been decorated lavishly by those intuitive PreRaphaelites. William Morris himself painted its organ. Carew effigies too make it a place to visit; one of their brasses has the Four Evangelistic (and Zodiacal) beasts at each corner, as if they knew where they were. The park must throng with distinguished ghosts - among them Sir Walter Raleigh, cousin to the Carews. They claim here that after his execution his body - without his head - was secretly buried in their vault, while his son kept the head at East Horsley. How apt, Gallant Sir Walter has laid the cloak of his headless body at the Virgin Queen's feet for ever.

Libra

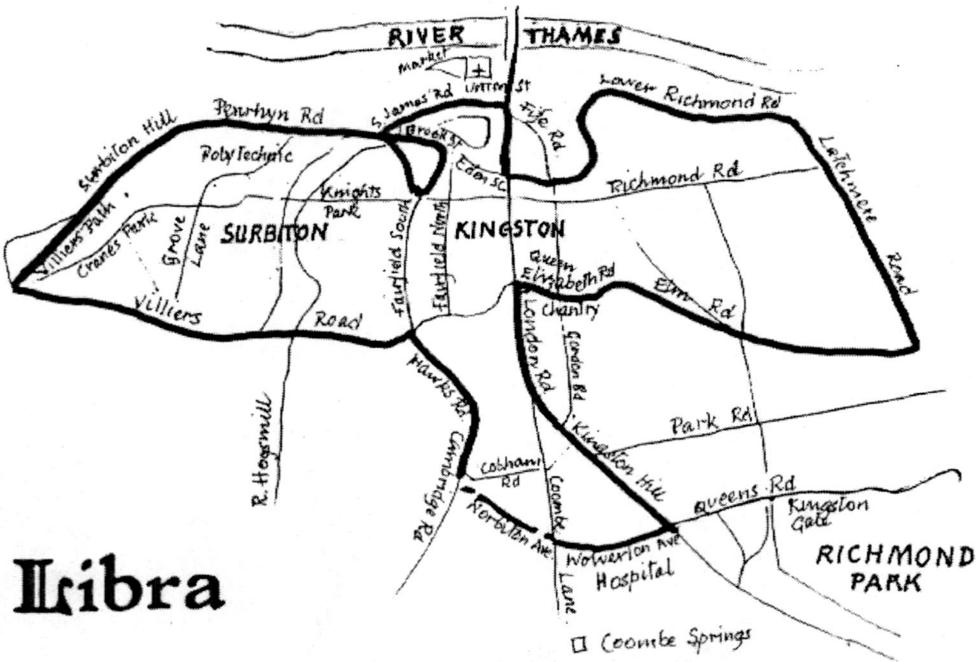
RIVER THAMES
Market
Lower Richmond Rd
S. James Rd
Fife Rd
Brook St
Eden St
Penrhyn Rd
Surbiton Hill
Polytechnic
Knights Park
Richmond Rd
Latchmere Road
Villiers Path
Cranes Park
Grove Lane
SURBITON
KINGSTON
Fairfield South
Fairfield North
Queen Elizabeth Rd
Elm Rd
Chantry
Villiers Road
London Rd
Gordon Rd
Hawks Rd
Park Rd
R. Hogsmill
Kingston Hill
Cambridge Rd
Cobham Rd
Coombe Lane
Queens Rd
Kingston Gate
Norbiton Ave
Wolverton Ave
Hospital
RICHMOND PARK
Coombe Springs

Libra

In the introductory chapter some of Libra's clues have already been mentioned; but there is more to say.This bird, its outspread wings governed by the Thames, its body at right-angles to them by reason of the bridge carrying the old London road across the river, nonetheless resembles the Libran Scales in shape. (It was possible to cross the Thames here long before the first bridge, as Kingston's earlier name, Moreford, " great ford," shows.) In other words, this bird' s basic form depends on Nature.

The Scales of Justice are much in evidence too on the walls of its magnificent County Court, erected about 1900, and quite the most distinguished of Kingston's more recent buildings. Alas, it has been found too small for later times, and is now redundant, its future uncertain, and replaced by a modern building next door. The word "Dove" appears in large letters just opposite both of them in Penrhyn Road - where intuitive soap-manufacturers of that name operate. Long may they remain!

It is strange that Surrey's County Courts should be in Kingston at all - for they should be in Guildford, long the County Town. (Common sense would argue that they were sited here because Kingston was nearer for London lawyers than Guildford; - but Zodiac buffs may wonder whether Kingston's Libran Scales of Justice were not more influential.)

But in these primaeval earth-and star Zodiacs we must not expect Libra to be signed by the Scales, which were only formed from Scorpio's claws in Graeco-Roman times. Glastonbury's Libra is a bird, at the centre of that Zodiac, displaced from Libra's normal position, and Kingston's bird repeats it. This aerial symbol, flying from the head of the sun-god Sagittarius the Archer like an arrow from his bow, is his fugitive spirit - The Holy spirit or Logos, borne on a sunbeam. In the Glastonbury Zodiac it flies south toward Virgo to quicken the womb of the ever-virgin earth, bringing the Creator to rebirth. In the Kingston circle it aims west at his Geminian son. It is at once the world-creating Word - the Dove of Noah, of the Annunciation, and of the Jordan baptism: indeed, this creative ray of inspiration still bombards us.

I couldn't find this bird myself, but one of my art students, seeing me struggling with the map, found it at once for me, with the scornful comment "Its all nonsense, of course.." As a Libran, I was abashed to realise that I was unable to find my own sun-sign - and was reminded of the saying in the Mysteries " Man, Know Thyself." But there it was, all drawn by Kingston's main roads. The only comfort I could draw from this humiliation was to realise that I lived on the tail of this bird, at the lower end of Kingston Hill. But I had only just caught it, by the skin of my teeth...

Is its beak the wedge-shaped market, grasping the Coronation Stone, its eye the parish church? Or is its head as on this map? It fan-tail revives the hospital on Kingston Hill; for just above, Wolsey Springs' medicinal waters flow under it. Cardinal Wolsey piped these springs, along with those on Coombe hill, to Hampton Court; both sets of well-houses can still be seen. Do these healing waters, passing as they do beneath this ever-growing hospital, account on the Feng-Shui principle for its success?

But is this Libran bird a dove? For there are many bird-candidates here; Cranes Park suggests another. Birds, being for millennia seen as messengers from the gods, have always been connected with letters. Hermes, said the Greeks, invented letters while seeing cranes in their V-formation flight. But even before him cuneiform had stamped its V-shaped image on Babylonian clay. Perhaps Hermes, being the first hermit, also watched cranes fishing - when their long curved necks and knock-knees would spell out the whole alphabet with no trouble at all. (Kingston's old Hermes Hotel still overlooks the Thames.) Druids, like the Greeks, held the crane sacred for its legible legs. Was Taliesin the Bard not inspired by immersion in the weir of Gwyddno Garanhir, the long-legged crane? Bards read these legs as I A (Jah), and said that "when God breathed His name all creation sprang into life - and one was the hearing and the seeing."

I into A made the Druidic Broad Arrow, once printed on convicts' clothing. It is still used on Government property today and suitably enough, is often found on hill-peak trig points. They called it the "Awen" - white - wings; its flight to earth made thought take form, the Word take flesh.

Many birds have expressed this IdeA. The Christian dove is the best-known, but the winged Logos is older than this, and its wings were not always white. Saturn sent faxes earthward by ravens which began as strips torn from the hem of his garment. The druidic wren came (like its name) from Urien - its cocked tail a seminal image of potent Uranus. Fitting so tightly into its round nest it suggested A into O, Alpha into Omega - or inspiration entering the world, the human head. Zeus too visited earth in various forms from swans to eagles, to fertilise earth-maidens.

So which bird casts its inspirational shadow over Kingston? Besides Cranes Park, its vanished Crane Inn and Crane Wharf favour Hermes' bird, while Eagle Wharf and Eden Street's towering stone eagle support Zeus.

The Three Pigeons pubs just off either wing-tip towards Richmond and Long Ditton suggest a dove -though this last has recently been demolished to make way for ever more car salesmen on the Portsmouth Road.

Is it a robin, flying west from the head of Sagittarian Robin Hood in Richmond Park; the Archer's arrow-bird, red-breasted from the dying sun? Or is it a gander, homing southward down Gander Green Lane to Maid Marion in Sutton's Sherwood Park? In the beginning was the Word, so all began with the gander - unless the gannet began it.

Is it a hawk? Hawks road helps to outline the bird's body. Or a hawk-headed Griffin? The old Griffin Inn still survives in Kingston Market, and though it is no longer an inn, it has kept its sign. (Egyptian Horus was hawk-headed, because he received the spirit of his dying father Osiris, and Katharine Maltwood saw the 2nd. Twin of her Glastonbury Zodiac as a Griffin-bird.)

Raven's Ait on the Thames presents us with yet another possible candidate. Celts saw the raven or chough as Arthur's spirit. An ark-like building covers this island, and Rocque's old map delightfully calls it " Raven's *Arse* Ait." Noah's last view of the raven he released from his ark, perhaps - or was it once Raven's Ark's Ait?

This stretch of river draws the prow of the boat that does duty for Cancer instead of the Crab in both these primaeval Zodiacs, so it is both Noah's ark and Jason's Argo. Castor and Pollux the Heavenly Twins were among Jason's crew, and Pollux the divine Twin of Molesey sits in it, endeavouring to pull his reluctant and all-too-mortal brother into it, to save him from sinking in his own iniquity. The Zodiac, source of so many ancient myths, has given this heroic Gemini figure in his boat many names, among them Noah (who with his sons saved the whole human race from extinction) - Ulysses, Jason,

Dionysus, Taliesin the inspired bard, and the Druidic Hesus or Esus, whose pre-christian name so remarkably resembles Jesus.

With such a rich choice of bird-messengers it is not surprising that Kingston has long been giving out the Word. Edward Gibbon learnt to write his " *Decline and Fall of the Roman Empire*" at the Grammar School. George Meredith, John Galsworthy and R.C. Sheriff lived here, to mention but a few luminaries. It is no surprise that Kingston has been the cradle for several local newspapers.

The little Chantry chapel, our oldest building, in its original state, seems to have begun a centre of education which is still expanding. Built in 1309 and endowed with a priest to say mass for the prosperous Lovekyn family who due to Kingston's three salmon fisheries were fishmongers to royalty, its influence has spread to two schools on either side of it in the London Road. Priests of these chantries had time to spare from praying for the dead, and often taught local boys until the suppression under Henry VIII, and many - like the Queen Elizabeth grammar School who owns the little Chantry - were refounded as secular schools by Henry' s successors, Elizabeth and Edward VI, thus salving their uneasy Tudor consciences.

As the Fair Maid of Kent sent her son Richard II to school in Kingston; it is certainly a possibility that he attended the Chantry school, before it was suppressed. Tiffins School opposite, in whose grounds the Chantry Chapel is situated, was a slightly later foundation. Both schools have earned reputations second to none. How could they fail? Kingston's feeling for education has since spread to both wings of its inspirational bird, and a large Polytechnic with a famous Art school has recently become a University that now bids fair to spread over its whole body.

Libra, ruled by Venus, favours the arts, and the town has two excellent galleries of modern art - the Stanley Picker collection and Dora Gordine's sculptures in her home Dorich House, now administered by the University. There is also an interesting collection of topographical paintings to be seen in the gallery of the lively Museum. (This collection, still ongoing, was instigated by Reginald Brill, artist and Head of the Art College he made famous, to preserve a memory at least of Kingston's many old buildings that have fallen victim to developers.) Venus, Libra's ruler, has not shone down on this town in vain.

And while we are in the Museum, we should inspect the Zoopraxiscope of Edweard Muybridge, the pioneer of moving pictures, who was born and died here. One suspects however that his ruling influence was pioneering Aries, Libra's opposite sign reflecting across the Zodiac. He was actually a sun-Arian, born April 9th.1830, travelled widely throughout the Americas, photographing among other things the building of the Pacific Railroad. (Aries is ruled by Mars, whose metal is iron.) Aries' martial spirit was too strong for him at times, for he shot his wife's lover dead, and was only saved from execution by a brilliant lawyer, claiming it as a crime of passion. It might be said that Libra the lawyer came to his rescue here.

But though the Libran Scales of commerce have been allowed to diminish Kingston's Libran charm, it has by no means totally evaporated. The Market Place can still boast several mediaeval buildings. The town was once a favoured holiday resort of Londoners like Jerome K. Jerome, who happily enjoyed its riverside beauty and hospitable inns, and it is still much sought after as a place to live. Its ancient market, whose statutes forbid any others to compete within nine miles of it, still survives - perhaps due to the influence of these commercial Scales.

Libra is an air sign, which may account for Kingston's notable aircraft industry. Though this has now dispersed elsewhere, its inspirational inventors materially helped our nation to survive two World Wars. From the Sopwith Camel to Hawker Hurricanes and Harriers, Typhoons and Tempests, these pioneers often laboured to produce planes at the eleventh hour - too often without Government encouragement and at their own expense - that could compete with aerial enemy intruders and overcome them. The Sopwith Camel actually used the Thames as an aquatic runway. What a magnificent bird it must have looked to watchers on the riverbank as it splashed down, swanlike, before their astonished eyes!

Those who know Libra as a peaceful sign may wonder at the thought of these birds of vengeance taking off from here - but Kingston has long housed the East Surrey regiment too. Are our aircraft pioneers a reflection from Libra's opposite sign, Aries the Pioneer, and the barracks ruled by its warlike ruling planet, Mars?

Perhaps, for it is a tenet of astrology that opposite signs can influence each other; but Mars and Venus in any case go together, as action and reaction, and Libra more than any other sign needs a partner to argue with, so in the absence of a friend an enemy will do. Astrologers have often observed how many generals are Sun-Librans. Perhaps it is no accident that General Eisenhower planned his World War II campaigns in Telegraph Cottage on Kingston Hill.

Libra equalises the sexes. 18th century Esther Hammerton is an outstanding example. When her father the sexton undermined Kingston's old Saxon church by digging a grave too near its walls, they were both buried beneath its ruins. She was the only survivor to emerge, and continued as the grave-digger in his place for many years. The Museum has a print of this robust woman, her beefy arms as strong as any man's. It is another curious fact that the only statues

Kingston could boast until recently are of women; the Shrubsole monument in the market, the marble Countess of Liverpool in the church, and the gilded Queen Anne on the Market Hall. (And even those notorious telephone boxes, though whether they can be counted as sculpture is dubious, at least reinforce the communicative nature of Libra.)

Lawyers and judges flourish under this sign, so perhaps it is no accident that the only recumbent effigy in Kingston Church is that of Sir Anthony Benn, an Elizabethan Recorder for Kingston and London. (His descendant is still arguing eloquently for social justice at Westminster.) And is it accident merely that Sir Thomas Hansard, the first editor of Parliamentary debates, is also buried here?

The Libran love of debate is well-known, but only men were allowed to indulge in it, so Kingston had a way of dealing with its argumentative women; it was long the custom to dunk scolds in the Hogsmill from the Clattern Bridge on a ducking-stool. This bridge, by the Coronation Stone, has kept its original Norman arches, and is one of the oldest still in use in the country. Some say that King John had a palace here beside the Hogsmill, where the Police Station now stands. King John's Dairy, a splendid ancient building nearby, was demolished alas in the 19th century, but a pillar from the palace was found and now stands in front of the Library, to remind us of when Royal Kingston was truly royal. It was King John who granted the town its first Charter.

The Saxon Dynasty, descendants of the fair and wise Alfred, several of whom were crowned on Kingston's Coronation Stone, were by and large Libran in their sense of fair play and justice - in contrast to their Norman conquerors. Their Witan of Wise Men sowed the seeds of our later democratic parliament, and though these remained dormant for oppressive Norman centuries, they survived in race memory until they eventually pushed their way through once more. I prefer to see this influence in making the Mother of Parliaments, rather than that of Simon de Montfort, who we are taught first granted representation in Westminster to towns and boroughs. For he was essentially a harsh and oppressive Norman, son of the Simon de Montfort who so cruelly decimated the Cathars of the Languedoc; and though he did indeed make parliamentary reforms, one suspects that such a man was using popular pressure to further the interests of the barons against the king.

This sign is small, but its influence has been great - and still spreading. Its Coronation Stone is more than a historic monument; it is a symbol of an ancient dream of fair and popular government, a dream that is still struggling to be realised, world-wide. In fact, crowning kings by popular acclaim on a stone was an old Celtic and Druidic custom before the Saxons came, as the Stones of Tara and Scone testify.

And though this bird represents the Letter or Word, it is the very opposite of the "letter of the Law" - rather its enlightening Spirit, without which law itself becomes all too often a hollow mockery, benefitting only lawyers. Libra is merciful, and the dove is the spirit of mercy, which alone can make the Balance true.

We should be grateful to Katharine Maltwood for discovering - or rediscovering - this bird in her Glastonbury Zodiac. Her effigy is partly outlined by "Dunstan' s Dyke," and thought to be an irrigation channel instigated by that perceptive bishop, who is so much in evidence also in Kingston. Not only did she rediscover Somerset's Star-Temple, most intriguing of earth Mysteries, but in recovering its earliest configuration restored to the Zodiac's battered mythical menagerie much of its original meaning in a form that clearly states its message.

For the incomprehensible centaur of Sagittarius becomes the Creator on his sun-steed, battling with darkness and chaos; apparently worsted nightly and annually, yet always rising renewed to seed the earth with new life, new ideas, by sending a sunray from his dying head - the Dove that replaces the Scales. Menaced by Scorpio's claws and sting at winter's onset, he is buried in Capricorn's wintry grave, yet resurrects as the Aquarian Phoenix or eagle after the winter solstice. Capricorn's horn is the latent cornucopia of next season's harvest, for the sun-god is a seed-god too, sleeping beneath Saturn's frosty shroud. The crested phoenix, reborn from the ashes of its self-made pyre, is a time-honoured symbol of the self-renewing year, and appears as Aquarius in some Roman Zodiacs.

These birds make two promises. The Aquarian Phoenix assures us that when we are ready we too will fly free of the Zodiac's recurring wheel of lives, to expand the universe in fields beyond our ken. Meanwhile the Libran bird descends from the heavens to earth, enlightening those still in semi-darkness, semi-consciousness, below.

I rejoice to find it reproduced in the right sign at Kingston's law - centre, “dropping like the gentle rain from heaven upon the place beneath”. Long may it inform our laws. For the very word Dove is an obsolete past-participle of the verb *to dive*. God “ dove” to earth, using this symbolic bird as messenger. More than one old Celtic poem begins “Duw Dovydd sends me a ray of inspiration ” -

Banishing the intrusive Waterman at Aquarius leaves only three human signs, in an equilateral triangle across the circle - revealing the Trinity of all ancient religions - Father, Mother, and Son. (The dual nature of Gemini, half earthy, half divine at present, is destined to become One; but more on this theme when we come to this sign).

The Christian Trinity is also implied, when the Dove of the Holy Spirit replaces the Scales.

Are not airy Aquarius and Libra better signed by birds? What Geminian would not take ship with the Son of God and Man? What Cancerian would not exchange the Crab for this ship, equally aquatic, more poetic - and able to ferry him to greater things? Under this restored Zodiac all myths, all faiths can unite, all sectarian squabbles dissolve. In its light even science and religion may come to terms; science agreeing that life and consciousness stream to earth from the sun - religion seeing its orb, ceaselessly immolating itself for us, as the visible regent of a benevolent Creative Force infinitely beyond our power to discern.

Scorpio

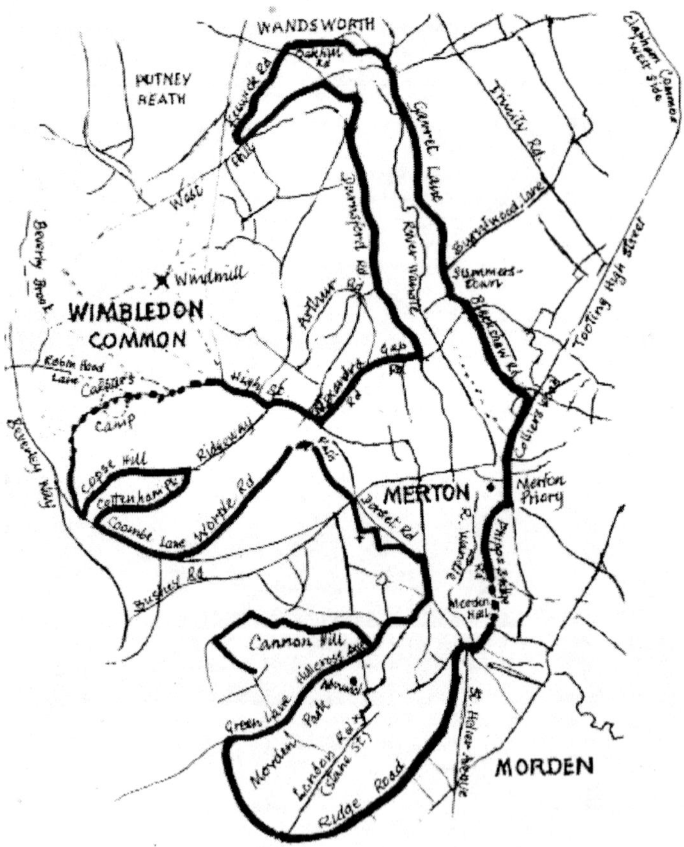
WANDSWORTH
PUTNEY HEATH
WIMBLEDON COMMON
Windmill
Garratt Lane
River Wandle
Trinity Rd
Summerstown
Tooting High Street
Durnsford Rd
Arthur Rd
High St
Gap Rd
Camp
Copse Hill
Ridgway
Cottenham Pk
Coombe Lane
Worple Rd
Dorset Rd
MERTON
Merton Priory
Bushey Rd
Cannon Hill
Morden Hall
Green Lane
Morden Park
London Rd
Ridge Road
St. Helier Avenue
MORDEN

Scorpio

"Here Scorpio, bent, its tail and arms surround a great extent:
In a wide circuit of the heavens he shines
And takes the place of two celestial signs."

So sang the poet Ovid. It seems symbolic that in his time (43 BC-18AD) that this sign should loom so large, when the Roman Empire had expanded over much of Asia and Europe--for Scorpio is ruled by both Mars and explosive Pluto.

Apparently it was only when things had settled down and the Pax Romana was established over this vast battleground that Libra's Scales were restored, being formed from Scorpio's claws to weigh the souls of the dead.

In the Kingston Zodiac Scorpio is also disproportionately large, overrunning Libra's domain - that sign being displaced in the centre of the circle, and as we have seen, in the form of a bird. As can be seen from Scorpio's diagram, I am in two minds about its tail. Does it run up the Wandle to curve round to its sting in West Hill, or is it bounded by Burntwood Lane and Tooting High Street, to curve round Clapham Common West Side? I leave it to you to decide...

Scorpio is the death-sign of the Zodiac, a character it acquired from about 4000- to 2000 BC, when Taurus and Scorpio were Equinoctial signs - Taurus "opening the year with its horns". Egyptians, when the sun declined in the opposite sign of Scorpio, floated the dead body of Osiris down the Nile in an ark, attended by his Mother-sister-wife the triple goddess Isis. (So Arthur, ferried in a barge mourned by three weeping queens to Avalon. Both sun-gods succumbed to treacherous relatives; Osiris to his brother Set or Satan, Arthur to his nephew-son Mordred.) Persians, incidentally, called November "Mordad" - Death.

Morden Hill in our Zodiac reveals a Scorpionic claw. Here Cannon Hill remembers Mars its ruler, and Roman Stane Street tramples through this effigy, laying down martial law. In fact, though peaceful enough now, this whole area was subjected for many centuries to cruel ravages not only from invading Romans, but afterwards by Saxons and still later by the Danes. Roman roads were a mixed blessing, for though they brought trade, in these disturbed centuries they were much used by armies, bringing fire, scorched earth, rape and destruction to all in their vicinity. Here Saxon fought Saxon, and Saxon later fought Dane. The Wandle was also a channel to this area for these merciless Vikings, invading by its means from the Thames. Ravensbury - mournful name - yielded 77 graves of c.500 AD, containing not only soldiers with their weapons, but mutilated bodies of women and children. Phipps Bridge had another such graveyard, and Tooting Graveney's name seems to tell the same sad tale. Much of our Scorpio still has a depressed air, as if it had never quite forgotten these successive periods of devastation. And as if the Romans, Saxons and Danes were not enough, William the Conqueror, when he was refused entry to London, decided to terrorise its citizens into submission by turning south down the Stane Street and devastating the land on either side of it, continuing in a wide curve round Surrey into Berkshire.

It is a notable fact that Scorpio's area contains more cemeteries, modern as well as ancient, than any other of this Zodiac's signs. Car cemeteries seem to abound too; Scorpio's metal is iron or steel.

This stern sign also contains one of our most well-known prisons - at Wandsworth. In Scorpio we pay for past failings, and being made painfully aware of them, are given the chance to wipe the slate clean.Does the Wandle remember these Vandals? Or does it derive from Van or Ban, the old Gaelic word for "woman" ? For the Wandle runs right through this sign to Virgo's skirt at Beddington.

Merton church as we have seen was founded by a Saxon who saw a shaft of light fall on the spot, and dedicated it to the Virgin. It is noticeable how Virgo tends to encroach here on Scorpio's domain, contesting it with him, aided by the Church, which-also built Merton Priory here. All men love virgins and fear death, and fearing it, prefer to forget it. Merton, earlier spelt Martin, may thus be either Mars' or Mary's town; here Mars and Mary meet, fight and marry. For this is where Saxon Kenwhal came in search of his Fair Maid - but unwisely forgot that behind her skirts lurked Kynard's Scorpionic dagger. Here Mars dies, and Mary survives the death-sting, for Merton church is full of widows. It displays a memorial of Captain Cook's widow, who tragically survived not only her husband but all six of her children. Another hatchment is of Lady Hamilton - Virgo at her most seductive - who outlived martial Nelson. A third hatchment on these walls also belongs to an unknown widow. It is interesting that two such eminent sea-captains had connections with Scorpio's water sign.

Nelson bought Merton Place from a William Hubbald; whose family estate here existed in 1500. (A *widow* Hubbard, doubtless a member of this family, fell on hard times and was maintained by Merton parish in 1775 at 2/ 6d a week. Was she the original Mother Hubbard of the nursery rhyme? They bought her a petticoat too. Not only her cupboard was bare, as a witty local historian remarked.) Nelson's mansion has gone, and his estate, once watered by the Wandle, is built over now. All there is to remember him by locally are Nelson's Fields, a little mounting-stone by the church fondly remembered as his, and the Nelson Arms in Merton High Street, depicting his Victory flagship on an exterior wall. Zodiac pilgrims should take a tot of rum here, surely, to toast the hero.

In Merton churchyard is a splendid Norman arch, thought to have been the Guest-house gateway to Merton Priory, and brought here from a mile away, where that great gem of architecture, *as large as Southwark Cathedral*, once stood, strategically placed on the crossing of the Stane Street over the Wandle at old Bradenford. A house was later built round this arch among the ruins after the Priory was suppressed under Henry VIII, fortunately preserving it until the house itself being demolished, revealed it once more..

Tragically, this is all that remains of this once-important Priory - unless we count the pathetic foundations of its Chapter-House. These have reluctantly - and I must say, inadequately - been preserved by Sainsbury's hypermarket, which now straddles the site. What a comment on 20th century values! Is this really the best that Sainsbury's could do, with all those millions to spare? Worse, a new dual carriageway, Merantun Way, now runs headlong down what was once the nave, obliterating a little sanctuary garden with an altar erected by archaeologists, which until recently reverently preserved this once sacred spot.

How many eminent characters passed beneath Merton churchyard's Norman arch? Kings were crowned, royal weddings were celebrated, and Henry III lay in state at the Priory - difficult though it is now to imagine such mediaeval pomp and colour in Merton's present industrial squalor. It takes imagination now to see mediaeval monks fishing for their Friday dinners in the Wandle, or to visualise those grey chevroned walls reflected in its now so murky waters..

This Priory played an important part in our history, producing such men as Walter de Merton and Thomas a Becket. Particularly interesting from our point of view are the Statutes of Merton, which in 1236 were enacted here to protect widows, minors and wards of Chancery from Scorpionic ravishment.Virgo, or Libra's lady of Justice, saving her own from Scorpio's claws!

Something has risen from the ruins, however, for William Morris that great artist, poet and social reformer, built his tapestry works here using some of the fallen stones, and Liberty's came to make their famous silks there. Their weaving and fulling sheds still survive, and are now home to the enterprising Abbey Mills Centre with New Age classes in such subjects as astrology. (Scorpio, who delves into hidden mysteries, is the astrologers' sign.) It is heartening to see this oasis flourishing from the ruins. You can eat there, browse among unusual shops selling things like rare sea-shells, and stroll along Wandle's banks with its old iron mill-wheel, towering above some intriguing modern outdoor sculpture. Take William Morris's " *News from Nowhere*" with you to invoke his noble shade. The battle for territory is apparent here too, for what could be more Virgoan than silks and tapestry - or more Scorpionic than an ancient priory trampled underfoot by industrial squalor?

Since Scorpio is ruled by Mars whose metal is iron, it seems peculiarly apt that the Surrey Iron Railway should have run the length of this sign. It was the world's first public railway, albeit horse-drawn, not steam-driven. It was inspired by coalmine railways, which had discovered that pit ponies could pull six times the number of trucks when they were on iron rails. Opened in 1803 and operating until 1846, it ran from a dock near the mouth of the Wandle down Garrett Lane to Summerstown, then by Mead Path to Colliers Wood and over Mitcham Common to Croydon, where there was a flourishing market. Its cargoes were typical of Scorpio's Pluto too - coal and dung. (Pluto rules anything mined from underground, and Scorpio has rule over the bowel and sex systems in the body.) The dung, stored in heaps as high as a house from London's many horses, was avidly collected at rural Croydon by farmers and spread over their fields. On its return journey the loads were equally typical of Virgo the Earth-Mother; stone and lime from the quarries of the North Downs to build London, and corn to feed its population. One hopes the trucks were thoroughly hosed down before they returned.

Scorpio is rich in past experience, deep soil for new beginnings. No wonder John Innes made his famous compost on this sign. He also pioneered genetics (that Scorpionic sex system again.) The sign is also secretive, occultly inclined, and Innes was an ardent Freemason, founding Merton's Lodge. During his long life he dominated the neighbourhood as its squire, and was something of a local dictator - another Scorpionic trait. His composting now continues successfully elsewhere, but his interesting house and extensive grounds have become a school, devoted to rearing young sprigs of humanity instead of plants and seeds.

Is Stane Street really no older than Roman? Very often they straightened and metalled earlier tracks, and the name Tooting on its course - *twt* in old Welsh, *tot* in old English, suggests an old lookout mound. If it is still there I haven't found it, but on the top of Morden Park's hill, on the southern claw of Scorpio, is another large mound on this old track, giving panoramic views. Should it not be excavated to find its age?

St Lawrence's church is nearby. This martyr, roasted alive on a grid, evokes Scorpio's hell-fires. "I'm roasted on this side, turn me and eat!" he taunted his tormentors. Only Scorpio dares laugh at death. St Lawrence's tears, a meteoric shower, fall like Lucifer from heaven.

Downhill, the Wandle threads through the delightful park left us by old Morden Hall. Morden, though sadly raped by the 20th century, has not entirely lost its charm; there were water-mills here too. The Wandle shows uncanny Scorpionic energy considering its short course through flat land, being able to keep so many mills turning in times gone by. Another water-wheel still survives near Carshalton Ponds near its source.

Scorpio's northern claw lies partly on Wimbledon Common, where Caesar's Camp and Well are a must for Zodiac pilgrims. Alas, experts now doubt that Caesar was ever there. Perhaps the word "seizer" suits this claw so well that the name has stuck, despite them. A landowner in the 1800s tried to build on it, but being refused permission, in fury levelled much of the camp's ramparts, so they are now but a shadow of what they were; but its rounded shape, raised around 300 BC, shows clearly from the air. At least the area round the nearby well was certainly occupied in very early times, for many neolithic flint arrowheads, knives and scrapers have been found there. There is also a large barrow near the Windmill, which R.W. Morgan in his intriguing book "*St Paul in Britain*" written in 1860, claims to be the grave of Guiderius or Gwythyr, Caradoc's brother, killed there fighting the Romans when they next invaded, some ninety years after Caesar. I heartily recommend this book, written by an erudite Welshman, though you will have to order it from the public library service as it is now out of print. It gives illuminating insight into this period of our island story usually skated over by most English historians, and he backs up his startling assertions with quotes from many contemporary Latin sources.

The camp stands 180 feet high on the edge of a plateau, so could easily be defended; yet when the Water Board cut a trench through it no skulls or weapons were found, bar one bronze axe from a far earlier period.

If evidence of battle is lacking, could it be that this ring had another purpose? Situated on Scorpio's claw with views to the south and west, might it not be a ritual centre to celebrate the dying sun-king not only for this settlement but for the neighbouring one too, equally ancient, at Coombe on Kingston Hill across the valley?

23 barrows were reported just south of Tibbets Corner in the 1700s, but these have all disappeared, being used to resurface the Portsmouth Road hereabouts. (Yet another of Scorpio's cemeteries.) Plainly this plateau was much occupied in earlier times. Robin Hood Lane climbs up to Caesar's Camp from Kingston Vale, Arthur Road (though this is a comparatively recent name) approaches it steeply from the eastern side, where Durnsford Road indicates an old crossing over the Wandle.

The constellation Ara - the Altar - occurs between Libra and Scorpio in the sky. So if Zodiac pilgrims want to contemplate the dying sun and invoke their ancestors here, there could be no better place than this delightfully rural spot. Camp Road leads right through it from Wimbledon village. But beware of stray golf-balls whizzing past, for part of the camp , though open to the public, is now a fairway for the local club. Safer perhaps to meditate by Caesar's Well nearby.

In the Glastonbury Scorpion two churches (one now a ruin) guarded the Zodiac's eastern water-gate at East and West Lydford, flanking the river Brue. Arthur's' funeral barge, they say, floated down it past them into Avalon - significantly enough through its death-sign. Two churches opposite each other on either side of a river is an unusual arrangement, but it is echoed on the Thames by Fulham and Putney churches on Putney Bridge, eastern entrance to the Kingston Zodiac. Mortlake's " death lake" is just beyond. Here Sagittarius and Scorpio meet, fighting their last battle, as sun-kings were wont to do, at water's edge.

Does the Oxford and Cambridge boat-race re-enact Arthur's funeral barge procession, itself an echo of the Nile funeral-barge of Osiris? True, the Varsity race has only been rowed from Putney to Mortlake since the last century, but before that it took place on the *Isis* , Oxford's name for its stretch of the Thames, where that university's Druidic foundations have long cherished ancient traditions. It may well have been rowed on London's Thames too in Roman times, for there was at least one temple there to the Egyptian goddess. The London Museum has more than one Roman flagon dredged up from its depths, inscribed "Fanum Isisi". Did Oxford's hot young blood jostle impatiently in past times for position, translating this once dignified mourning water procession into a race? Its present course, by strange coincidence, bounds the figure of the Sagittarian sun-king.

Giant effigies generate giant legends. Boack's 18th century "Middlesex Antiquities" records that two giant sisters built Putney and Fulham churches with but one hammer between them, tossing it over the Thames when one shouted "Put nigh!" and back when the other cried "Full Home!" When the hammer fell awkwardly and broke its claws an obliging Hammersmith nearby mended it for them. Does neighbouring Hurlingham also remember these hurling sisters? It is tempting to see them as Libra and Virgo, and clawed Scorpio as the hammer. The Smith? Who but the grumpy giant Wayland, the ill-tempered 2nd Twin of Weybridge? For his father and mother the Giant Wade and his wife Bell also built two castles with only one hammer between them, throwing it back and forth to each other. And though this is said to have happened far away near Whitby, two giant sisters built St Martha's and St Catherine's chapels on the Wey near Guildford in the same cack-handed fashion. Our 2nd Twin lies between the rivers Mole and Wey; South Weylands Farm is on his effigy, so there is some justification for identifying him with Weyland.

Bishops of London have occupied moated Fulham palace since Saxon times. Why so far from the London of those days? Was it to guard this water-gate to Kingston's Zodiac? Fulham church, dignified by this long line of bishops, is full of interest. Its quaint carving of an Elizabethan lady is only one of several treasures that will reward a visit. And were those prehistoric stones at Fulham Palace's mediaeval gate thrown there by the hurling sisters? They look like Kingston's Coronation Stone; were all three once part of a lost stone circle?

Or was Weyland responsible? He is famed for throwing one at least a mile, hitting a cowering imp at Snivelling Corner from his Smithy on the Oxfordshire Ridgeway. The stone is still there to prove it. No doubt he was busy at the time shoeing the Uffington White Horse nearby. Like our 2nd. Twin, he was an irascible giant; and if you think he was incapable of travelling from Whitby to Hersham via the Ridgeway, you have forgotten those seven-league boots.

Scorpio has some famous characters, notable among them being Thomas Cromwell who was born in Putney. His father was a notorious rogue, a drunken bully more than once imprisoned, not only for assault but also for forging documents. Thomas escaped from this unpromising start as soon as he could by going abroad and made a fortune, first as a merchant and then as a moneylender. He became Cardinal Wolsey's secretary, and somehow surviving his master's fall, succeeded him as Henry VIII's chief adviser, steering him through the legal jungle of divorcing Katherine and marrying Ann Boleyn. Pragmatic and worldly-wise, he survived until he advised the much-married Henry to wed Anne of Cleves for political reasons. Too late, Henry found he couldn't stand this “Flemish mare”, and blamed Thomas. Catholic enemies saw their chance and accused him of every crime they could think of. (Cardinal Pole called him an “emissary of Satan” - a truly Scorpionic title.) Henry, who had made him Baron Wimbledon, failed to support him, although he had faithfully fulfilled his promise “to make him the richest prince in Christendom” by overseeing the Dissolution of the Monasteries and giving him their accumulated wealth. So Thomas went in his turn to the block. It is ironic that from his Wimbledon seat he could look downhill and see the stones of the noble Priory he had ruined, being carted away to make Nonsuch Palace..

Interesting too that as the architect of the revolution known as the Reformation, he was the great-uncle of Oliver Cromwell, another Scorpionic revolutionary. At least in Thomas's favour it must be said that it was he who ordered a Bible to be read in English in every church in the land - a privilege hitherto unknown, and fiercely resisted by Catholics of his day. Historians and those who want to trace their ancestry must always be grateful to Thomas for insisting that every church must henceforth keep a record of all births, deaths and marriages in the parish. Until then, only those who could afford the expense had the privilege of recording their existence in church memorials. Cromwell's ordnance was a sign that even the plebs from now on were beginning to count - a sign that the old feudal chrysalis was cracking open, and a new individuality for all was emerging. If few could read, at least they were read to in church in their own tongue, a mind-opening process; they were to be educated, and even the main details of their lives, however obscure, were now to be recorded for posterity.

The Cecils, who helped Elizabeth steer England through another crisis, the Catholic threat of the Armada, also came to live at Wimbledon. Sir Thomas, later Lord Burghley, her Secretary of State, rented the Old Vicarage. His eldest son Robert who followed him as chief adviser to the queen, built the great manor house in the late 1580s. Grand though it was, entertaining a succession of the great from Elizabeth to James 1st, the Old Vicarage has outlasted it to become Wimbledon's most distinguished ancient building. Long may it survive. Thomas had carefully trodden the tightrope of Mary's bloody reign, attending mass devoutly as long as it was required. The Cecils, Machiavellian in their guile like Thomas Cromwell, were just what Elizabeth needed at this turbulent time. Wimbledon has played a great part in the establishment of England's Tudor Reformation. They lived here for over 100 years, and the church, though suffering much rebuilding, still has their interesting memorial chapel.

Though the Cecil's immediate forebears came from Stamford, they proudly traced their ancestry back to the Sitsyllts of Herefordshire, an old Welsh family that goes back through immense reaches of time to two kings of Britain called Sisillius, who appear in Geoffrey of Monmouth's king-list as coeval with Solomon and Hiram, about 900 BC. Presumably from Sicily, this sounds as if they were Phoenician in origin. The Cecil's' brief reappearance on the political stage seems a fateful reincarnation at this critical period of our national fortunes - for after that the family retired to Hatfield's splendid Tudor mansion and took no further part in state history. Clarendon wrote witheringly "their wisdom and virtues died with them", and says that Robert's son "was a man of no words, except of hunting and hawking." Pepys called him " my simple Lord Salisbury."

The Tudors, conscious of their Welsh ancestry themselves, gathered many of their countrymen to court to stimulate the Tudor Renaissance with their Druidic heritage of history, music and poetry. The Welsh contribution to this sparkling cultural period has been greatly underplayed. It is interesting to find poetic Lord David Cecil in our own day reviving this bardic strain.

Later, the Spencers occupied Wimbledon Manor. The 2nd Earl being First Lord of the Admiralty until 1802, must have been responsible for the promotion of Nelson, his neighbour at Merton at another critical time for England during Napoleon's threatened invasion. (The noble arch surmounted by a stag near the church must date to this period, and is all that now remains of the great house. It was pulled down and rebuilt more than once) Though this earl disapproved of Nelson's liaison with Lady Hamilton and gave the pair a cold reception when they returned from Naples, his choice was inevitable, for Nelson had already proved himself an outstanding sea captain. Nelson's character must have had something of Scorpio. Though he was a sun-Libran with all its charm, his passion not only for women but for renown, his magnetism that bound his seamen to him, his utter fearlessness and consequent wounds in battle, are all typical of Scorpio. So is his jealousy which consumed him while at sea, fearing that some notorious buck might cast lascivious eyes upon his love left unprotected in England. He could be cruel too; insisting that his wife shared the house with them on the occasions when he was home from sea - until unwilling to take any more humiliation, she left forever.

One attempted Scorpionic seizure (like Caesar's) should appear in these pages. An 18th century Earl Spencer tried to enclose a part of Wimbledon Common to enlarge his estate, at a time when many landowners were doing it. (Those claws again) But fortunately for us all, the locals, also stimulated by Mars and Pluto, opposed him, equally determined not to lose their ancient rights to feed their animals on the Common, and pulled down the fences he had erected. So bowing to popular pressure, he withdrew his claim.

Southside House, opposite the old Crooked Billet, has some truly Scorpionic relics to show for its fascinating history. It is older than it looks, being originally a farmhouse. The Royalist Thomas Pennington lost his son in the Great Plague of London of 1665, and took the house, then far from the city, for the safety of his surviving family, enlarging it in the popular Dutch style of his day. The first relic this house can boast is the vanity case and comb with which Anne Boleyn made herself ready before going to the block on Tower Hill.

Sir William Carey had married her sister Mary, and led Anne out on her last tragic walk from her cell. After the execution (for which she requested a sharp sword, not the usual axe) -

he collected these sad effects, which came by marriage into the Penningtons' possession.

A later John Pennington who must be the original Scarlet Pimpernel, was at the English Embassy during the French Revolution, and was able secretly to help several aristocrats escape from the guillotine to England. He was given a rare relic in gratitude. This was the pearl necklace which had fallen from Marie Antoinette's neck when she was guillotined. It had come into the hands of Napoleon's Josephine, but when the Emperor heard of it he was horrified and wouldn't have it in his palace, so she gave it to John for having saved some relatives of hers.

The Wharton family married into the Penningtons. Nothing more Scorpionic can be imagined than the notorious Duke Philip Wharton, who was often at Southside House. He was outlawed for conspiring to reinstate the banished Stuart Pretender to the throne, and for indulging in black magic and general debauchery. At a time when the aristocracy were famous for their licentious behaviour, apparently he fell below even their standards. He was a member of the notorious Hell-Fire Club of Medmenham Abbey and West Wycombe Caves, when a young girl was seduced and died in the orgies, and an old lord had a fatal heart attack as a result of one young rake jumping on his shoulders from behind, dressed as the devil.

There is a pastel of this tearaway Duke -(who can help wanting to see him?) and another of his widow, who came to live at Southside after he died disgraced in Spain.

Among the many portraits is one of James Stuart, Charles 1st's nephew, whose father and George Wharton killed each other in a duel. A Stuart plaid and the sinister relic of George's rapier still hang above it.

One last Scorpionic treasure must be mentioned before leaving this tragic house of history; it is the great sapphire of the Russian Romanoffs, shaped like a fig and set in diamonds. Given to John the Scarlet Pimpernel by a grateful French refugee, it became the Pennington talisman, as it had been the Romanoffs'.One hundred years later in 1893 John Pennington-Mellor's wife wore it at a royal ball in Athens, where it was recognised by Olga, a Romanoff who had become queen of Greece. It was at once offered back to her, but she refused to take it. This was perhaps unwise, in view of the Romanoffs' later tragic fate in the Russian Revolution. Though this fateful jewel was not on display, there was a signed photo of Queen Olga on a table.

These are but a few of the treasures of Southside. In a way that merely reading history cannot, they have the power to touch the heart and bring us close to the characters who suffered these Scorpionic tragedies. Interested parties can book a guided tour by writing to the Administrator, the Pennington-Mellor Trust, Southside House.

Scorpio is the sign of "fixed water." A contradiction in terms, one might think; but the great engineer Sir Joseph Bazalgette, who lived at Wimbledon, managed it, curbing the Thames' spreading tides and periodic flooding by designing and building its Embankments. He also greatly benefited Londoners' health by carrying out the city's vast drainage system, excavating some 83 miles of sewers - a truly Plutonic activity, bearing in mind that this sign has rule in astrology over the body's eliminative system. This great work was opened in 1865; until then what sewers there were had drained into the Thames, whose consequent pollution and potential for disease had become a growing cause for alarm.

He also built Battersea and Putney bridges, and designed a tunnel under the Thames near the Tower, but died before he could excavate it. He surely deserves his monument in

Wimbledon parish church. Like Merton's John Innes, he worked on Scorpio's constructive side.

Another who struggled all his life to combat one of this dominating sign's worst evils was William Wilberforce, who fought tirelessly against all odds to outlaw slavery. He came from Hull, being orphaned at the age of eleven, and lived with his uncle and aunt on the edge of Wimbledon Common. On his marriage he went to live at Clapham, (still on this sign), but returned to inherit his relatives' house when they died. His unpopular campaign to ban the slave-ships plying from English ports to American plantations lasted fifty years; it needed Scorpionic courage and those tenacious claws to oppose such a long established and profitable custom, even though he was aided throughout by the younger Pitt. They were great friends, Pitt often strolling across the Common from Bowling Green House on Putney Heath to see him. But even a Prime Minister's help couldn't overcome the powerful vested interests in Parliament, and it was only shortly after his death in 1833 that the final bill abolishing the trade was passed. Nor was this his only humanitarian cause; though an evangelical Christian, he battled for Catholic Emancipation, for Parliamentary Reform, and for the establishment not only of Sunday Schools but general education for the children of the poor. Buried as he deserves in Westminster Abbey, he too justifies his memorial in Wimbledon church.

Lord Dowding who lived in St. Mary's Road is another of the intrepid inhabitants of Wimbledon who have helped to save the country in desperately dangerous times. Yet another of Scorpio's heroes, he was Leader of the Few in the Battle of Britain. He and his wife, deeply affected by the deaths of so many young men in that aerial conflict, became keenly interested in Spiritualism - another Scorpionic preoccupation - and wrote books on the subject. But more than writing in the normal way, he was responsible through a medium for several messages in automatic writing from those who had died in the war to their still-living relatives; a revelation which caused a profound stir at the time. He also found that he could help bewildered dead souls to pass to the other side in peace. His courage in the face of much resultant ridicule was equally Scorpionic, and left him undaunted.

Lord Dowding, Sir Arthur Conan Doyle and Lord Baden-Powell are but three of the many distinguished visitors to Wimbledon's Spiritualist church. But earlier still in 1934 the famous medium Estelle Roberts opened her House of Red Cloud (named after her spirit guide) in Wimbledon's Hillside. Although this closed in 1941, Hillside has the reputation of being the most haunted road in the district. More than one house there has reported ghosts and other strange happenings. You can read of these - and many more - in two intriguing booklets called "*Mysterious Wimbledon,*" by Ruth Murphy and Clive Whichelow, to be found in local bookshops; they certainly bear out the town's Scorpionic and Plutonic vibrations. Not only it seems has it more than its share of ghosts, the Theatre and the Windmill being the scenes of several reported sightings - but it also has more than its share of underground tunnels, and infamous murders; both the dark domain of Pluto. And on the subject of tunnels, I must not neglect to mention the most impressive one of all; the Underground Northern Line from Waterloo, which enters Scorpio at Tooting Bec and ends at Morden on his southern claw.

The authors also list a number of notable duels fought on Wimbledon Common. (What can be more Scorpionic than this?) Two of them involved Prime Ministers, no less. The younger Pitt fought George Tierney in 1798, though luckily for England's fortunes neither was wounded, and the duel was stopped. Later Lord Castlereagh challenged George Canning and shot him in the thigh. The Duke of Wellington was another important figure in the history of this period who hazarded his life here in a duel and fortunately for England's future, survived.

I am indebted to these books for learning about another noted psychic who lived in Wimbledon - the journalist and author W.T. Stead, who was drowned with the Titanic in April 1912. But twenty years earlier he had written the novel "*From the Old World to the New*" about a ship which sank through hitting an iceberg in the Atlantic. And even earlier he had penned a short story involving a liner that went down with much loss of life, because too few lifeboats were provided. Strange premonitions of a watery Scorpionic death! He had been warned too by a medium that he would die by water, and that April was a month when he was especially vulnerable. In view of all this, it seems incredible that he risked the voyage But one gets the impression that he was aware that this was his fate, for survivors report that when everyone else was crowding panic-stricken on to the inadequate number of lifeboats, he was last seen calmly reading a book in the stateroom.

It is in Scorpio's November that we look back on the past and remember, remember. Not only the saving of Parliament on Guy Fawkes' - (yet another national crisis) -- but now the millions of dead in two World Wars. So it seems significant that on this martial death-sign the parishioners of Wimbledon, not content with the usual commemorative plaque or village cross, have dedicated a whole War Memorial Chapel to them in their church...

Sagittarius

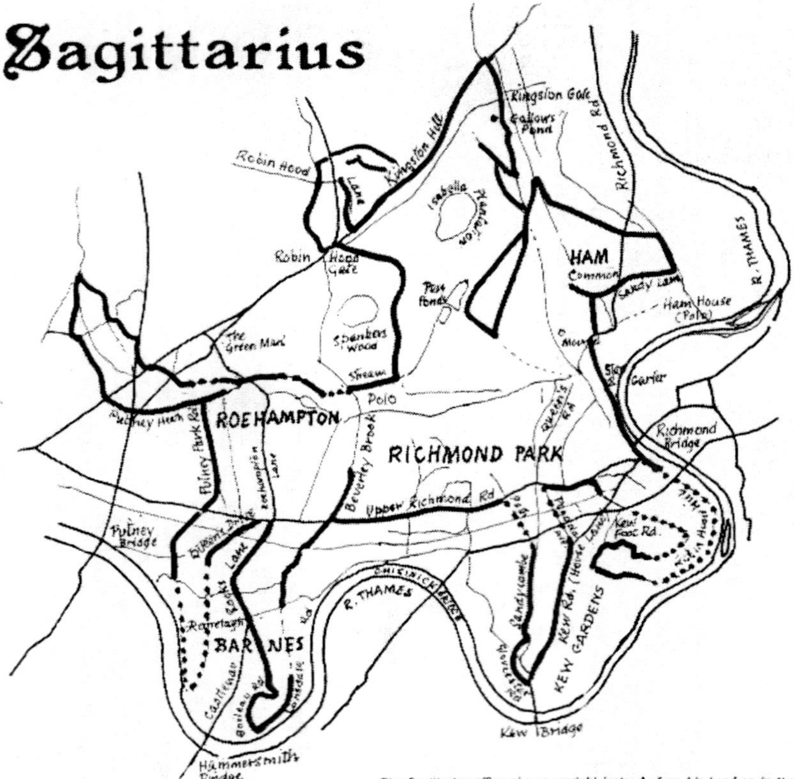

The Sagittarius effigy shown upright instead of on his head as in the circle

Sagittarius

This December sign, identified since Assyrian times with Ahura or Assher the sun-god, hangs upside-down on all the maps of Richmond Park, as on the Zodiac. In fact the very shape of the Park marks his pointed helmet or hood at Kingston Gate. Before Christ divine saviours have hung this way, descending vertically to earth and thus making a cross with its horizon. "Nine days hung I on the tree Ygdrasil" said the Norse god Odin. Ygdrasil was the giant ash that bridged the worlds from its roots in the underworld to its topmost branches in the heavens.

Sagittarius, though centaur-like, is here a mounted archer, drawn by roads and footpaths across the park; his bow, the Thames' curve, aiming for the stars - specifically the Bull's-eye star Aldebaran(Taurus' red eye) at well-named Strawberry Hill just across the river. The paths that draw Sagittarius' figure so dynamically are ancient, for they led to old villages and settlements long before Charles I finally enclosed this area as a royal hunting ground.

It is remarkable how bends in the Thames allow for his horse's head and legs. Is the Archer helmeted or hooded? Arthur or Robin Hood? Arthur Road on his helmet near Kingston Gate would seem to identify him with the Glastonbury Zodiac's Sagittarian hero, but Robin Hood Lane and Gate, and Robin Hood Hill, marked on old maps in the Old Deer Park on his horse's front leg, plead for Robin, the people's Saxon champion. Parallels between both archetypal saviours have already been touched on in the first chapter; and both belong more to myth and popular ideals rather than history, so perhaps we need not choose between them, or exclude either. For both essentially represent the sun-king who lives, battles and dies for his people.

The sun-king's story varies from country to country and from one time-period to another, but certain similarities recur. His origins are often obscure, so he begins humbly - being either born of a virgin or rejected by his royal father because seers have predicted that his son will eclipse him. Noble but unrecognised, he has to prove his innate superiority by some notable feat in youth. Only Arthur could draw the sword out the stone - Robin overcame the mighty Little John, and could split a wand with his arrow at a prodigious distance. The sun-king gathers a loyal band about him, and outwits or overcomes superior forces arraigned against him. He rescues the poor and disadvantaged, reinstates the dispossessed, punishes the unjust, and generally shines benevolently on all. But he is nevertheless betrayed, often by a woman, sometimes by a trusted follower, and killed. Like the sun however, he is expected to return.

This effigy appears to be hooded, so remembering the hooded mummer on his hobbyhorse in the Robin Hood Games in mediaeval Kingston and mindful that Robin was an outlaw, I was struck by the fact that several outlawed highwaymen once operated on his figure - among them the theatrical Jerry Abershaw who ravaged Kingston Hill, Wimbledon and Putney Heath. He was the highwayman who has a sign erected to him on Tibbett's Corner, whisked by the horse's tail. He was caught in Southwark at the ripe age of 22 and hanged, laughing and joking even on the scaffold; his dead body was strung up on Wimbledon Common on a barrow near the windmill known ever since as Jerry's Hill.

Nearby is the old Green Man Inn. Surely this great effigy must be Robin in Lincoln Green, for his acres covering Richmond Park, Barnes Common, Ham Common and Putney Heath are uncommonly and surprisingly green. Commuters speeding south-west over Putney Heath may see the high plateau of his body in the wooded hill looming before them as they descend into Kingston Vale.

Archery is still practised in the Old Deer Park and the Roehampton end of Richmond Park, and the archer/outlaw himself dropped me a delightful hint as to his identity, when armed with these clues, I naively ventured to persuade the curator of Kingston Museum that he was there. A qualified archaeologist, she was in a difficult position, but bore with me politely until to her great relief the door opened to admit a postman, with something in his hand.. It was a neolithic flint arrowhead that he'd dug up that morning in his garden. Would she like to have it for the Museum? "Of course" , she said - "Where is your garden?" Inevitably, it turned out to be in Robin Hood Lane. What timing! The Archer's own arrow - what could be more pointed? It was only the next day that I realised I had been trying to persuade Maid Marion of the existence of Robin Hood in her own manor - for Marion was indeed her name....

The Zodiac can play enchanting games with those who search for them. Questing the Virgin at Merton church, I found three fresh Arum lilies recently dropped (from a coffin, no doubt) and lying on the churchyard path for me. Incredible that such expensive flowers should be left unnoticed on the ground - but there they were - a gift it seemed from Virgo herself.

On another occasion a newspaper reporter who badly wanted some sensational copy interviewed me at home. Was I a witch? Alas, I couldn't claim to be. Didn't I have a coven with nude nocturnal rituals? Again, no. But though I showed him the Kingston and Glastonbury Zodiacs and tried my best to enthuse him, he went away, bitterly disappointed. That week I took a friend to explore Virgo, and whom should we meet in Nonsuch Park but this same reporter! Astounded, I pointed out to him that we'd met on the Witch of this Zodiac - but even this weird coincidence failed to impress him, and I never saw him again. Both time and place were giving him what he sought, but to him it was just a meaningless coincidence..

Am I being pixie-led? For Robin king of the witches, and Robin Goodfellow of folklore whose band of elves are green and hooded, are older far than Robin Hood. And if there are none at the bottom your garden, I am persuaded that you may see the king of them all in Richmond Park.

Was Sagittarius the mounted archer drawn in effigy in Britain *before* he became the centaur of Babylonian and Greek Zodiacs? For a mounted hero by bad copying over time could easily become a centaur, but hardly vice-versa.. Sense can become nonsense, but the reverse is less likely. Arthur dragged forward over his mount's neck by the Whale in the Glastonbury Zodiac makes good mythical sense - being the sun-king dragged in winter into the sea, or below the horizon. The dynamic rider of Richmond Park leans forward in the same way, so that his body fuses with his mount's up-reared neck. Could these two star-temple figures be nearer the original Zodiac concept than the monstrous centaurs of old? For centaurs, with the single exception of noble Cheiron, the teacher of young heroes, were monstrous in character too.

Richmond Park's shape outlines in its southern part the head and shoulders of the Sagittarian rider, and there are many clues to his presence. His eye is Gallows Pond, as befits a hanging figure on the Zodiac, though it was named no doubt from the gallows on which highwaymen used to hang - on his shoulder; on the crest of Kingston Hill. His domed forehead rises just inside Kingston Gate, an eminence where Zodiac pilgrims may sit, and facing west, contemplate the gloriously setting sun. Mark how the road from Kingston Gate to Richmond draws his profile, delineating his nose as it bends round the western boundary of Thatched Lodge, where a sandy excavation marks his nostril. The map on the Park

Gates will not help here, for it (inaccurately) makes this road straight.

His heart-is *heart-shaped* Isabella Plantation, just where it should be, and blood-red with rhododendrons and azaleas in spring. No-one seems to know who Isabella was, so why not see this as the sacred heart of Ysu-Bel? Life-giving streams have formed his ever-potent penis at Pen Ponds, amid scenery worthy of Bel or Baldur the Beautiful. Spankers Hill (another name otherwise unexplained) spanks his horse's rump! Though its back is difficult to trace now with certainty, there was a green road from White Lodge which led over the Beverley Brook by a still-existing bridge through what is now a peoples' golf-course to an entrance in Kingston Vale with the mind-boggling name of Chohole Gate - *near its tail.* Make what you like of that.. Roehampton Lane and Dover House Road delineate his buttocks and hind legs through Rocks (Hock's?) Lane, helped by the Beverley Brook, the stifle joint, until they disappear in Barnes reservoirs.

The Star and Garter just outside Richmond Gate is by its rider's knee - a fitting home for heroes, overtaken like Sagittarius by wintry old age. And at Sheen, where the rider's heel should be, is the Spur Inn - or was, for it has now closed. There is a common-sense reason for this name, for it is on a railway spur; but it is yet another strange coincidence. The horse's head is drawn by a road through Ham Gate, and is shaped by Ham Common. Queen's Road leading up to Richmond Terrace was earlier called Black Horse Lane, and the Kew Road that draws the mount's front leg, also appears on Rocque's old map as Horse Lane. Black and White Horse Inns recur all over this figure; even the "Maltese Cat", a tavern in Roehampton, is named after a polo pony made famous by Rudyard Kipling; and the splendid Spotted Horse of Putney High Street caps them all.

Polo is only played in Richmond Park and at Ham House, and nowhere else on this Zodiac. This royal game requires a centaur-like capacity to be one with the pony's sudden twists and turns. Richmond Horse Show too has long demonstrated the area's preoccupation with this noble animal, and though it has recently closed down, there is popular pressure to revive it. Equestrians gallop round the park in increasing numbers, for hiring stables flourish all about it. The bent foreleg of the Sagittarian horse is clearer on Rocque's old map, which traces it across the Old Deer Park, its hoof aptly enough at Kew Foot Road. The road or path delineating it once led to an observatory in Georgian times, where society of the time thronged to observe the stars. It is here on the Thames that older maps show “Robin Hood's Hill” - a suitable place indeed for archery.

Richmond and Kew have always been royal, and the identification of Sagittarius as an outlaw may seem to be at odds with this. But we are reckoning without the wide-ranging character of the sign, which is ruled by expansive Jupiter, “the greater benefic.” With a humorous twinkle in his eye, he is on easy terms with all men, whatever their station, so long as they are not mean or vindictive. (You must admit that some of the place-names on this figure betray his sense of humour.) Loving all sports, especially horsemanship, he must have sympathy with highwaymen, especially gallant ones - realising that they were often disbanded soldiers, turned loose by an ungrateful country, their war service unrewarded.

Sagittarius' 9th. House of Higher Mind in its upper reaches is that of the sage, the philosopher-king. Looking beyond the worldly glory of Leo, king of beasts, his sights are set on higher things, questioning the human predicament, the very meaning of life. Kew observatory, while it lasted, was symbolic.

Katharine Maltwood assigned Leo in her Zodiac to Lancelot, peerless in arms but limited by his all too earthy love for Guinevere, which prevented him from achieving the Grail, try though he might to find it. Her Sagittarius was Arthur, a philosopher-king indeed, for his vision encompassed the Round Table of Chivalry, from which the knights set out on the otherworldly Grail-Quest. And it was Robin Hood's vision of social justice that transformed a mob of dispirited outlaws into a merry band devoted to righting the wrongs of the dispossessed.

So it is satisfying to find that some well-known philosophers lived on this sign - Bertrand Russell, whose father the visionary Lord Russell of Pembroke Lodge worked tirelessly for parliamentary reform - and Elizabethan Thomas Hobbes of “Leviathon” fame, who was tutor to two generations of the Earl of Devonshire's children at Roehampton House.

Truly philosophic too was the author J.G. Bennet, who founded the Institute for the Comparative Study of Man at Coombe Springs on the crest of Coombe Hill in 1946 - near enough to Sagittarius to be under its influence. He bathed daily in one of the two Wolsey Well-houses that were in the grounds of the Institute. (Had those waters a spiritual power to illumine the mind?). Bennet was a pupil of that extraordinary Armenian mage G.I Gurdjieff, and propounded his philosophy. I attended many lectures there and found them a mind-opening experience; in fact I was among many who regarded the place as an esoteric university during the 20 years it lasted. It was designed to last for ever; one of its foundation clauses stipulated that it could not be sold. But alas it was not to be. Bennet eventually gave it over to the Sufis and removed the Institute to Sherborne. Before long Coombe Springs was closed, and its beautiful grounds sold for building. But at least Bennet's books are in Kingston Library. And those who want to learn more of Gurdjieff's ideas, drawn as they were from the accumulated wisdom of many hermits, monasteries and ashrams in the Middle and Far East, must read "*In Search of the Miraculous*" by P.D. Ouspensky, Gurdjieff's chief pupil. (The impulse to learning on Sagittarius seems compelling, for Kingston University has now spread to perch on his shoulder on Kingston Hill.)

Visit Pembroke Lodge in the Park, where you may be refreshed on its terrace and enjoy the superb and much-painted view that must have inspired Bernard Russell. And while there, don't fail to visit Henry VIII's Mound in the grounds. From its size and commanding position on a high ridge overlooking the Thames one feels that it is probably a prehistoric lookout mound for a vanished British Camp. From here one can see across the landscape to Windsor Castle, looking west; eastward, when London's polluted air permits, St. Paul's noble dome appears. A swathe has been cut through the trees to allow this strangely inspiring sight. They say that Henry momentarily paused from his hunting in Richmond Park to watch from here for a smoke-signal to tell him of the execution of Anne Boleyn in the Tower.

Richmond and Kew both had palaces - Richmond's dates from mediaeval days. Under its Gatehouse - all that remains of glories that once vied with Nonsuch - ghostly hoof-beats can still occasionally be heard. These they say were made by the impatient horse of Thomas Carew, that shameless opportunist who waited for Queen Elizabeth to die in the chamber above, so that the royal ring could be taken from her finger and dropped to him, so that he could gallop with it all the way to Scotland and be first to curry favour with her successor James I. (Or are those ghostly hoof-beats a strange echo from the Sagittarian hoof at Kew Foot Road?)

But Elizabeth came late in the list of royalty that favoured Richmond. The distinguished aura of this effigy began (in records at least) with Henry 1, who had a manor at Shene. It is suspected however that this may not have started with him, and that the Saxon kings of nearby Kingston may have been there before him.

Henry III enlarged this hunting-lodge, and Edward I and his queen Eleanor often visited, watching tournaments held on what is now Richmond Green. In Edward III's time it became a regular royal residence; his queen Philippa of Hainault died there - Edward scandalising the court by giving her extensive wardrobe and jewels on her death to one of her maids, Alice Perrers, who was also his mistress. This redoubtable lady managed to live on after his death at Shene Manor, achieving respectability at last by marrying Sir William de Windsor.

Richard II, Edward's grandson, loved the place, and he and his queen Anne of Bohemia enlarged it further as a summer retreat with such extravagance that he became unpopular, and the resentment of London's citizens was only subdued by her charm. When she died there, Richard who loved her dearly, cursed the place, vowed never to visit it again and ordered it to be pulled down. But before the demolition got far he was himself pulled down by the usurper Henry IV.

Henry's son, the Fifth of that name, loved the manor and restored it. He built a monastery nearby in what is now the Old Deer Park to try and expiate his father's murder of Richard. He also founded a Brigittine nunnery of Syon across the river in gratitude for his astonishing victory at Agincourt, when with a rain-soaked handful of men with sodden bowstrings he somehow defeated the proud chivalry of France. It is this convent that later moved to Syon House at Isleworth. His son Henry VI often held court at Shene, its rural peace suiting his sensitive and pious nature. But it was no time for sensitivity; he was no match for the warring barons of the White and Red Roses, and his crown was usurped by Edward IV, whose tournaments on Richmond Green were famous for their magnificence. When Edward died aged only 42 his crook-backed brother wrested the crown from his son, the boy-king Edward V, and shut him up in the Tower with his younger brother - a fate from which they never emerged. But despite all Richard III's murderous attempts to eliminate all rivals, he was himself defeated at Bosworth by Henry VII. An emigre Lancastrian whose Welsh blood not only ended the Plantagenet dynasty; his tactful marriage to Elizabeth of York allied the warring Red and White Roses together. Peace at long last descended on England, and Henry Tudor, notorious for his economies, founded a new prosperity out of the ruined kingdom.

This was soon reflected at Shene, for when the Manor burnt down it was under Henry VII that it was totally rebuilt as a palace. Elizabeth of York had lived there as a child and loved the place; so no doubt it was she who persuaded him to rebuild it. Parsimonious he might be elsewhere, but no expense was spared on it. He was adept at raising money; "Morton's fork" , as his ingenious new taxes were known, caught his subjects on one prong, even if the other failed. And as he was the Duke of Richmond in Yorkshire like his father before him, Richmond Palace it became.

Here he entertained poets, musicians and philosophers, so that it became a centre for the Tudor renaissance in England. His daughter Margaret was married there to James king of Scotland; and there his short-lived son Arthur celebrated his marriage to Katharine of Aragon. After Arthur's untimely death, she pleaded to be allowed to live on at Richmond, and this she did until she married Henry VIII, and he took over Hampton Court. Shene Palace as old prints show was a wonderful sight while it lasted - and it lasted until the Commonwealth, when it was finally despoiled and sold. In the great days of Elizabeth, Shakespeare was summoned here more than once to perform his plays before her. Although she lived mostly in London, she was addicted to hunting at Richmond, and it was here she would summon Dr. Dee from

Mortlake to foretell her future and indulge her love of astrology.

Though by Hanoverian times the old Palace had gone, the Georges still favoured Richmond. George II who as Prince of Wales quarrelled with his father and was evicted from Whitehall, came to live at Richmond Lodge in the Old Deer Park. Court life here revived once more; Maids of Honour Row on the Green dates from this time. His son Frederick lived at Kew but died before his father; it was his wife Augusta who devoted her life to making Kew Gardens the world-famous place it is. George III, "Farmer George", approachable and amiable, and the first of his line to become popular despite his subsequent bouts of madness, removed to the Dutch house in these Gardens, thus extending the royal Sagittarian aura northwards. Two of his sons lived on Kew Green.

This long royal tradition here has gathered many great and splendid mansions to it and an air of civilisation and culture that still persists to this day. George's wife Queen Mary was born at White Lodge in Richmond Park, and Princess Alexandra, Duchess of Kent occupies Thatched Lodge.

The aristocrats that clustered round the Court vied with each other in patronising the arts in all its forms, so that architects, artists, poets, musicians, playwrights and actors were attracted to it. Geoffrey Chaucer even had a Court position there in earlier days. Johann Christian Bach, son of his famous father Sebastian, had a house on the Green. The first theatre was opened on Richmond Green by Garrick; the witty playwright Sheridan lived here briefly, and Edmund Kean lived and died next door to the theatre he loved. And when it finally closed it was soon replaced by the present one. Joshua Reynolds and Peter Lely had houses here; Gainsborough and Zoffany are buried in Kew churchyard. But the list of notables is endless - these are but a few of the luminaries attracted here by Jupiter's benevolent ray...

Though the aristocrats who drew them here have mostly gone, many of their mansions remain, erected at a time when architects knew how to embellish the landscape. Some, like splendid Ham House, are now open to the public, while others have found new uses as seminaries or been taken over by successful actors and pop stars. Richmond's charm is likely to endure, for its basic advantage is the steep hill overlooking the Thames's elegant curve, which gives such expansively Jupiterian views right across to Windsor and the Dorking hills. This famous prospect has been immortalised in many paintings and poems - not least in "*The Seasons*" by Richmond's own i8th century poet James Thomson, who lived in a cottage where Richmond Hospital is today. He is buried in the parish church, and Thomson's Pond in the Park's Isabella Plantation remembers him.

Typical of Sagittarius' independent mind was the beautiful but intimidating Duchess of Queensbury, of whom many tales were told. Disputing the ownership of a strip of land between her and her next-door neighbour the Earl of Dysart at Ham House, the intrepid lady seized a stick and drove him from the field. She refused to follow the fashions of the day, whose ladies she complained "curled their hair like sheep." A sheep she certainly was not. She championed the poet Gay, who had scandalised both Court and Government by lampooning them in his opera "Polly." She even stood up to ill-tempered George II on his behalf, and when the opera was banned, re-published it herself. As a result she was banished from Court; but responded by saying that this suited her admirably, as she had only attended out of duty, not from pleasure, and that if the king couldn't stand plain-speaking he would in future only be surrounded by sycophants. Horace Walpole, who lived opposite across the river, said "Thank God the Thames is between me and the Duchess of Queensbury!"

Sagittarius' open and enquiring mind often finds itself ahead of staid orthodoxy. William Harvey who discovered the circulation of the blood, lived at Roehampton, near the philosopher Hobbes. The two were great friends, and both were well-known locally for eccentricity.

Sagittarius is also the sign of long journeys; the saying "Travel broadens the mind" typifies it. Interesting then to find in Petersham churchyard the tomb of George Vancouver, who sailed round the world with Captain Cook and named Vancouver Island. (Another Sagittarian characteristic was betrayed by a parson of Petersham and Kew, by the horsy name *Colt*on, who earned notoriety in the 18th. century for compulsive gambling - winnng £2500 - a fortune in those days - in one heady night.)

Richard Burton, another indefatigable traveller, lived in his youth at Maids of Honour Row from 1821-41, and went to school in Richmond. Sent down from Oxford for "bad behaviour", he joined the East India Company and showed a remarkable talent for eastern languages. A swarthily handsome man, he dared to visit Mecca disguised in Arab costume and lived there undetected for a whole year - an adventure which would have meant death, had his nationality been known. In 1857 he went with Speke to discover the source of the Nile - a mystery of great European fascination at the time. But Speke cheated him while he lay in a fever near their goal, and instead of caring for him, went on alone to find it and take the credit. His triumph was short-lived, for when the furious Burton returned and summoned him to a confrontation at the Royal Society, Speke shot himself the night before he had to appear - whether by accident or design has never been established. But psychologists may well wonder... Burton's later travels covered Brazil, Damascus and Trieste, where he was successively British Consul. He also made expeditions to Iceland, Cairo and India. His broad-minded interests in the thought of other cultures resulted in his famous translations of the "*1001 Arabian Nights*" and the "Kama Sutra".He and his faithful wife, who endured unimaginable hardships travelling with him, lie aboveground, according to his eccentric wish, in a stone replica of an Arab tent, placed (as she was a devout Catholic) in Mortlake's Catholic church cemetery. Some of his writings were too broad-minded by half for her taste, and she burnt them before they could be published..

Another notable Sagittarian eccentric was Lady Hester Stanhope, brilliant niece of the younger Pitt, who kept house for him at Bowling Green House on Putney Heath. After his death the intrepid lady travelled in Arabia with Bedouin bands and finally settled among the Druses of Lebanon, whose mysterious teachings intrigued her. (Did some of their ancestors come to Britain long ago as Druids?)

Here she founded an ashram for anyone attracted by these ideas, which surely ranks her as a philosopher too. Her commanding personality and her reputation for divination gave her great power - pashas came to implore her aid. She was a great nuisance to the English government, being sympathetic to the people she'd adopted, and inveighing against English influence in the Middle East. So when she asked Parliament for financial help in her old age it was denied, and she died alone, in poverty among the mountains.

Her uncle, England's youngest Prime Minister at the age of 22, surely deserves the title of philosopher too for his visionary statesmanship. It was he who counselled George III's government to take a more liberal view of the rebellious American colony - saying "Be to her faults a little blind; be to her virtues very kind". Had his advice been taken, it is arguable that the American War of Independence might never have happened.

Another, if not eccentric, at least highly imaginative woman, much beloved of the people, was Queen Caroline, the ill-used wife of George II at Kew Palace. She must have been philosophic in outlook, for she enjoyed the friendship of Leibnitz. Though a German like her husband, she seems to have adopted with some enthusiasm the root-myths of Britain, for she built a grotto called Merlin's Cave in Kew Gardens. Under a triple vault sat the Druid sage with a large globe, visited by four figures of uncertain identity except one, Britomart (Britannia?) - come to enquire their destiny. Were they waxworks, forerunners of Madame Tussauds? No-one knows now, for they have long disappeared, and even the site they occupied has been forgotten. But at the time they caused a great stir and many poems of the period mention them. I for one, lament their passing. Was this an intuitive leap on her part? For Merlin belongs to Capricorn, just across the Thames from Kew.

Dr. Dee, a reincarnation of Merlin if ever there was one, lived at Mortlake on the northern edge of Sagittarius, but facing Capricorn across the Thames. He was a philosopher, scholar, mathematician and inventor who took the Tudor world by storm with his lectures and books on Euclid's geometry, seeing it (like Pythagoras) as secretly revealing the basis of harmonious creation - a Cosmology which included the influence of the stars. His mechanical inventions were before his time; while still a youth at Cambridge he astonished the undergraduates by making a scarab beetle which somehow flew upward with tiny human figures on its back “to fly to Jupiter”.Later he staged shows of “mirabilia” to fill his purse which must have been like our more sophisticated conjuring performances, with lights, hydraulics, mirrors, optical and perspective illusions and dramatic chemical reactions, which gave him among the ignorant a reputation as a black magician. Consequently when Queen Mary fell ill, he was falsely accused of afflicting her with spells, and cast into prison. Influential friends eventually secured his release as no evidence against him could be found, and on Mary's death Edward Vl made amends by giving him a pension. He made a horoscope to fix a favourable date for Elizabeth's coronation, and she often consulted him on astrological matters, promising him preferment. But this promise was never fulfilled - perhaps because he fell for the wiles of the plausible Edward Kelly, who offered by scrying in a crystal ball to raise spirits who could impart universal secrets to them.

He took Kelly into his house, much against his wife's will, and spent years being duped by the unscrupulous Irishman. Dee's weakness, his greed for secret knowledge, made him credulous of all Kelly's invented “visions”. But the indigent Kelly (who had previously lost both ears in the stocks) had found himself comfortable lodgings and was simply after material gain, hoping to wrest the secret of the philospher's stone from his master to make himself rich. The crystal ball is now in the British Museum.

On Dee's earlier reputation they travelled on the continent for some years, meeting many learned men. They were well received in the Bohemian court, where the Rosicrucian Enlightenment was in the ascendant - (see Frances Yates' book of that name) - and Renaissance philosophy was coupled with the invention of ingenious mechanical devices after Dee's own heart. It is said that he also acted as Elizabeth's secret agent while abroad, his code number 007!

Soon after they returned home Dee's wife who hated Kelly, fell ill with symptoms suggestive of poisoning. She had long suspected him of fraud. But it was not until she died that the scales finally fell from Dee's eyes, and suspecting that Kelly, under pretence of administering medicines to her, had got rid of this obstacle to his ambitions, he faced him with his treachery and threw him out. But his reputation was indelibly tainted.

By now in penury, his money spent too lavishly on old rare books and alchemical apparatus, he was rescued by Elizabeth. Towards the end of his long life he was given the post of

Warden of Manchester College - well away, one suspects, from Court life. But after nine years he returned to Mortlake, dying in 1608 after four years in great poverty, at the age of 81. It was a sad exit for one with such auspicous beginnings. Elizabeth had called him "her philosopher," and Aubrey described him as "one of the ornaments of his Age". But like Merlin, he was deceived by one who wanted to wrest his spells from him.

Capricorn

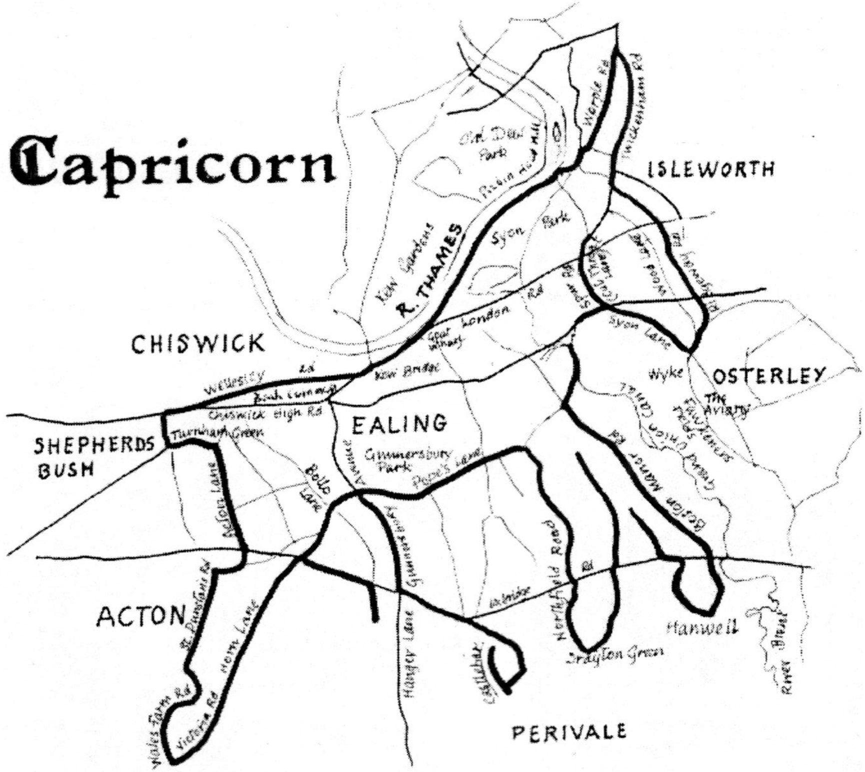

ISLEWORTH
OSTERLEY
CHISWICK
EALING
SHEPHERDS
BUSH
ACTON
PERIVALE
R. THAMES
Kew Gardens
Syon Park
Twickenham Rd
Wood Lane
Syon Lane
London Rd
Kew Bridge
Chiswick High Rd
Turnham Green
Gunnersbury Park
Pope's Lane
Bollo Lane
Acton Lane
Horn Lane
Victoria Rd
Wales Farm Rd
Hanger Lane
Northfield Road
Drayton Green
Hanwell
Boston Manor Rd
Grand Union Canal
Wyke
The Aviary
River Brent

Capricorn

There is a marked character contrast as we cross Kew Bridge from royal Sagittarius to busy, workaday Capricorn. When I first encountered Brentford High Street some years ago it was old, decaying and forlorn. Much rebuilding has been done since, but the architecture has made no effort to compare with its southern neighbour across the river.Capricorn in astrology is subject to delays and obstructions, and motorists attempting to cross this bridge know all about that. But they are by no means the first to be frustrated. A pillar erected in the High Street tells how even victorious generals were made to pause as they attempted to battle their way over Brentford's historic ford.

It records that here Cassivelaunus blocked Caesar's advance, Edmund Ironside delayed Canute, and Prince Rupert defeated the Roundheads, at least temporarily, at the Battle of Brentford. The large number of flint arrowheads and other prehistoric weapons dredged from the Thames here show that warring tribes faced the same problems at this point long before recorded history. It may console impatient motorists on Kew bridge to reflect that it was even more difficult to make this crossing in earlier times - and that there were many didn't make it at all. How many skulls and crossbones lie beneath the serene surface of the water?

An old and cryptic phrase, “the two kings of Brentford” mentioned by Thackeray as “sitting on a single couch” is thought to be an ancient memory of the ding-dong battles between Canute and Edmund Ironside, who crossed back and forth through this ford until they were finally reconciled. They also appear in a play by the duke of Buckingham, “smelling at a single nosegay". But they are both history and myth - for the new Aquarian sun-king also defeats his ageing Capricornian rival of the winter solstice at a ford, in more than one Celtic tale.

Almost opposite this stone pillar is aptly-named *Goat* Wharf, a notable clue among the once busy wharves on this reach. Nearby the Grand Union Canal, having brought goods from right across the country, empties into the Thames. Capricorn works hard for his living, and names like Commerce Road and Occupation Road here proclaim it. You won't find *them* on Sagittarius. Even Brentford's old church is now a furniture warehouse; no time for prayer, it seems. Which is odd, for astrologically Capricorn is the Priest, the Counsellor. At least Syon Abbey was once on his arched neck, to remind us of this facet of his character. Both he and Sagittarius, having attained the dizzy heights of the Zodiac's midheaven, are idealists that have gained wisdom with a strong religious bent, though Capricorn's faith is traditional, orthodox, while Sagittarius' conclusions are free-ranging, philosophic, and can be heretical.

Back Lane is on Capricorn's back in Chiswick, near where Turnham Green turns his hams down Horn Lane; his spine is the old Roman road westward from London to Staines.. So he has an iron ramrod of a backbone - something he needs to gain eminence (which he often does) from hard early beginnings. Indeed, strong bones are typical of this sign, which has to do with enduring structure and form. (Picasso's goat sculpture emphasises the animal's essential boniness.)

Chiswick House, peerless example of pure classical form, was built here by Lord Burlington from an Italian original in Vicenza called the Villa Capra. Strange - for Capra means she-goat!

Chiswick was named from its famous cheeses, and a crazy local tale insists that he faced this lovely Palladian building with Swiss cheeses - and only when wind and rain washed them away was the present structure revealed. In other words, only the Capricornian bones are left. Swiss cheese is often made with goat's milk, too. Wander in these lovely grounds, dignified by sweeping cedars, with an Ionic temple reflecting in a pond from which a stone obelisk rises, irresistibly reminiscent of Capricorn's horn. Sheltered by yew hedges are ancient stone busts brought from Italy - among them Caesar and Pompey. A 2nd. century Roman tombstone forms the base of another obelisk. Surely only on antiquarian Capricorn will we find such gems. And when you explore the villa's interior, don't fail to see William Kent's painting of the Zodiac!

Capricorn's graceful head, drawn by Syon Lane and Ridgeway road,noses Osterley's Aquarian hill just as Glastonbury's Capricorn's nose presses against the Tor's hill of inspiration, transfiguration, resurrection.

Is Osterley *Easter-ley*? Goats and men need mountains to climb, and ambitious Capricorn's motto is Per Ardua ad Astra.. His hind leg springs from industrial Acton. At Wales Farm road on his hoof, St Dunstan had a friary. Here is Pan, oldest of nature-gods, half - goat, half-man - and the River Brent perhaps remembers him as Bran, oldest of Celtic gods. Brentford used to be called Brain-ford. Capricorn is sentient life throughout evolution; which has slowly worked its way through the aeons from an amoeba to evolve a human brain. He only seems to have one horn here, which makes him also a unicorn, in whose horn is stored all our long-inherited instincts and hard-won knowledge; wisdom including the subconscious and superconscious, the mind beyond the brain..

Saturn, old Father Time, rules Capricorn; and Bran, who corresponds to Saturn, had a cauldron which rejuvenated the sick, weary, aged - even the dead. Osterley's rounded eagle to whom he aspires, is strangely cauldron-shaped. Is it not the rejuvenating Grail? If it seems contradictory to see the Templar emblems of Unicorn (soul) and White Hart (spirit) in this satanically horned, cleft-footed creature, the dichotomy already exists in our cloven nature. The Quest of the Grail, White Hart, Unicorn, all symbolise our need to unify our sundered consciousness.

The river Brent which bounds the front of this effigy, actually cuts his head from his body; it is the only place in the Zodiac where this happens. Does it symbolise the human situation? Only we among all the animals, suffer a forlorn sense of loneliness - of being cut off from Nature. No wonder every prince of folklore sought the Unicorn and the White Hart in the depths of the forest. This division, essential at first to develop the sense of individuality which distinguishes us from the rest of the animal kingdom, has over millennia developed dangerously, producing mental, physical and social ills, even threatening human survival - and the ecological survival of our planet itself.

Hartington, Hartham and Hartland roads here all tend to confirm Capricorn as the White Hart. So what magical impulse made Lord Hartington come and live at Chiswick House? The same no doubt that impelled Lord St Leonards to live on Leo. And speaking of place-names, how does Bollo stream and bridge on Capricorn's most potent part grab you? Alas, the stream has recently been primly piped underground to give way to flats, called (nostalgically) Brook house; but Bollo Lane is still there to remind us. This Zodiac has no inhibitions, as we noted on Sagittarius.

Nearby on the goat's belly is Gunnersbury Park, which may also appeal in this context to the subconscious. However, there is a legend that explains the name as the seat of Gunhilda, Canute's daughter. A later king's daughter also lived in this beautiful mansion - George II's princess Amelia. It is another oasis in built-up Capricorn, well worth a visit with its classical temple reflecting in water, a Gothic folly beside a second lake, and a museum with ancient artefacts from Brentford. A rich collection of coaches and carriages belonged to the Rothschilds, who lived here from 1735 for two or three generations. Curious that this pre-eminent Jewish family should live on this sign, for Saturn rules both Capricorn and the Jews. In fact, ardent Zionists did their best to buy Syon house at this time (also on Capricorn) - attracted by its name.

Antiquarian Capricorn, suitably enough, is rich in museums. The Music Museum in Brentford High Street is a riotous experience for young and old, with Fair organs playing at full pitch, automatic violins sawing away without human aid, and other wonders. The Steam Museum is nearby, with its powerful steel engines working away to entrance young engineers. And Syon Lodge's Garden of Antiques, if not quite a museum, is nevertheless a delight for lovers of old sculpture and other rare objects, all for sale.

Ealing on Capricorn's barrel derives its name from the Saxon "eolh" or Danish "Jelen" both meaning elk or eland; odd in the extreme, unless they knew of the giant creature beneath them. But perhaps Capricorn especially favoured giant elks in earlier days. The name later changed, absurdly, to Yelling. Rocque's map rather prudishly spells Bollo Bridge as "Bellow" too. With all this yelling and bellowing it is no wonder that Haven Green is a haven no more. Yet its name echoes Havyatt - "Gate to Avalon's haven" - on Glastonbury's Capricorn. And parts of Hanwell on the goat's front hoof still have charm, with its old well that has given the place its name, church high on a steep cliff looking down on the winding river Brent below, and its common, marked with stones on old maps. Was there once a stone circle here on this cliff-fortress?

Capricorn usually uncoils from a sea-shell, recalling life's primitive watery origins; but this goat (as in Merton College's Zodiac) has four legs. He needs these to support the Royal Coat of Arms as the Unicorn. *North Pole Junction* on his hind leg at Acton proclaims his wintry polarity to Leo's summer Lion - to whom his single horn points, across this Zodiac. The royal Secret is blazoned for all to see on the Lion and Unicorn Gates of Kew Gardens on the road leading from Richmond to Capricorn across the river. True, these are fairly recent 18th. century reminders of Kew's royal palace, but Merlin's Cave in the gardens also makes one wonder. Was Hanoverian Queen Caroline who had this made, intuitively on the wavelength?

For Katharine Maltwood assigned Capricorn in her Glastonbury Zodiac to Merlin the Druid magus, repository of ancient wisdom and adviser to Arthur. In one of his legends he wears a sickle round his neck, like Old Father Time. His name *Mer*lin seems to indicate that he like Capricorn emerged from the sea. Despite his wisdom he was something of an old goat too; for he made the mistake of falling for the enchantress Vivien and revealing his magic secrets to her - whereupon, tiring of him, she used his own spells against him, and immured him for ever in an oak.. An awful warning to ageing philosophers? An allegory of Druidic wisdom still springing green from the forest? Perhaps both... The lusty unicorn of legend was the strongest of all forest creatures, so ferocious that the only way to capture him was by guile. If you sent a pure virgin into the forest he would become quite coy and lay his horned head in her lap - and could then be netted with ease...What does this legend mean? What does it *not* mean? Interpretations vary from the bawdy to the sublime. Primitive Man civilised by love? Samson betrayed by Delilah? Merlin by Vivien? Is the virgin a sorceress, or the Bride of Christ? On one level it doubtless hints at one of Capricorn's characteristics - for like the goat, he is easily sexually aroused.

If Merlin sleeps in Acton's Oak Town he probably sleeps in oak sleepers now - his dreams shattered by railway wheels as they roar through Druidic Old Oak Common. The original grove must long ago have rotted away, giving place to Wormwood Scrubs. (What a Capricornian name!) He is not the only one to be imprisoned there, on this sign of delays and frustrations. It is no accident surely that two of our most well-known prisons occur on the two "malefic" signs of Scorpio (Wandsworth) and Capricorn. "Hard labour" must be one of Capricorn's watchwords.It is a disturbing thought that some are imprisoned wrongly. And Capricorn can be the Scapegoat - loaded with the sins of others and sacrificed to atone for them. 17th. century Boston Manor, from which Charles I watched the Battle of Brentford; has a painting of just such a sacrifice - of the ram caught in a thicket that saved Isaac from Abraham's knife. The original scene of this sacrifice, Mount Moriah, was Jerusalem's Temple Rock, the Hill of Zion. Curious that Syon Abbey on Capricorn's arching neck once owned Osterley's hill, making it too a Hill of Syon. No accident either that Spur road, curving round Capricorn's throat, was once called Cut-Throat Lane; it appears as such in Rocque's old map. Moreover, it leads up to the Gillette razor-blade factory on the Great West Road!

Splendid Syon House with its extensive Park on Capricorn's proud neck, is yet another oasis on this sign. But it has a woeful history that makes the decapitating Brent and Cut-throat Lane strangely apposite. The list of notables who were hanged, beheaded or imprisoned from here is tragic.. While it was an abbey one of the monks was quartered, drawn and finally hanged (in that horrible order) at Tyburn, for refusing to acknowledge Henry VIII as Head of the Church of England. The vicar of Isleworth parish church just outside the Abbey grounds was also executed for the same reason. Henry's queen Catherine Howard was imprisoned at Syon until she went to the block in 1542. In 1547 Henry's coffin, resting here on its way to Windsor, burst open, and dogs licked his blood; thus fulfilling the prophecy of the monk Peto. (As we have seen, this gruesome legend was also told, suitably enough, near the Dog of this Zodiac.)

The Duke of Somerset, (the Lord Protector of young Edward VI) was granted the Abbey after its suppression and rebuilt it as a Tudor mansion. But he was soon executed for treason, and it passed to his triumphant enemy the Duke of Northumberland, who fearing Catholic Mary Tudor's accession, engineered the crowning of this daughter-in-law, the reluctant Lady Jane Grey. But she only lasted nine days before Catholic nobles instated Mary in her stead, and she sent Northumberland, Lady Jane and her husband in their turn to the scaffold. "Bloody Mary" reinstated the nuns in 1547, but died the next year, and Elizabeth soon dissolved their abbey once more and banished them abroad. Thomas, the 7th. Earl, was a fervent Catholic and took part in a northern rising to replace Elizabeth with Mary, Queen of Scots, and was betrayed to Elizabeth, who promptly had him beheaded at York. The 8th. earl was imprisoned three times in the Tower on suspicion of the same sympathies, and was found there, shot through the heart. Whether this was murder or suicide was never revealed.

We have already met at Great Fosters the 9th. earl, known as the Wizard Earl for his interest in astrology and alchemy - (shades of Capricornian Merlin and his Northumbrian mentor, Bleise). He had his pitch queered in the reign of James I by Thomas Percy, a relative who was involved in the Gunpowder Plot, and unfortunately visited him at Syon the night before it was discovered. As a result the wizard earl, who was only interested in esoteric studies, was falsely implicated, fined £30,000 - a ruinous sum in those days, and because even he couldn't afford to pay it, was imprisoned in the Tower for 17 years. There he befriended Sir Walter Raleigh, a fellow-prisoner, and they spent their time smoking, casting horoscopes and conducting experiments that included distilling spirits, so their time was profitably - even bibulously- spent.

Zodiac researchers will be delighted to see a Unicorn supporting the Percy Arms on the large map of Syon hanging in the Portrait Gallery; the reason presumably being that it was the armorial beast of the earls of Suffolk, one of whose daughters married the 10th. Earl Percy, who had this map made in 1635. Capricorn's head and horn can be traced on it, and Osterley's Phoenix at its base - also Aries, Taurus' head and the two Fish at Heston and Cranford. This last is just visible on the far right. But as this map is not orientated north-south, the viewer must compensate accordingly. Those who want to study it more closely can buy a copy here, or at Osterley's shop.

After the poor Wizard Earl of Northumberland, Fate seems to have relented until the male line died out, leaving the child Lady Elizabeth Percy as sole heir. But she too seemed fated. Married aged 12 to the sickly Earl of Ogle who died in two years, she next married the wealthy rake Thomas Thynne of Longleat. But a rival who had his eye on her, Count Konigsmark, had him assassinated, was tried for murder, and managed to escape abroad in disgrace; so he failed to get her after all.. Her third marriage (while still only 15 years old!) was to the Duke of Somerset, who became President of the Council under William III. Known as the "Proud Duke", he proved too arrogant for George I, and had to resign his office. Marriage with him could hardly have been easy. It is a strange quirk of history however that Syon House through him came back to the house of Somerset, who first owned the Abbey after its dissolution.

The Proud Duke' s grand-daughter, Elizabeth Seymour, married Sir Hugh Smithson, who was a handsome but a man of cultured taste. Under his responsible stewardship Syon's fortunes revived. He employed Robert Adam to make the wonderful interior we see today, and Capability Brown to design the grounds. He was made 1st *Duke* of Northumberland in 1766, taking the name and arms of Percy. His natural son founded the Smithsonian Institution in Washington "for the increase and diffusion of knowledge among men." Though he'd fought under George III to try to keep America, his sympathies must have been with the colonists. But they wanted no favours from England, especially from one who was illegitimate, and it took ten years before their President John Quincy Adams persuaded them to accept the bequest. It is pleasant to recall Smithson's generosity to the USA, when we remember Carnegie and other benefactors to us from the New World. (Oddly enough, the Adams family who produced two American Presidents, came from Barton St. Davids, on the Dove of the Glastonbury Zodiac..It was at this period that the esoteric symbols so redolent of secret teachings appeared on dollar notes. And their descendent Evangeline Adams became famous for teaching astrology by radio all over the United States. The Dove it seems has flown across the Atlantic to spread the Word.)

Before we leave Capricorn, it is worth remembering that the young Vincent Van Gogh, a tragic figure if ever there was one, lived for a short time in Isleworth, teaching languages - and while there fell in love with his landlady's daughter. But his youthful pangs went unrequited, so Capricorn was not a happy experience for him. There is a blue plaque on the Georgian house commemorating this brilliant son of sorrow.

It is a curious coincidence that the Garvin family who lived later in this same house on Capricorn's horn, sold honey made in Glastonbury. In fact, it chimes in quite uncannily with Greek myth - and I am grateful to my old friend Ron Henderson for pointing this out. In the old tale, the goddess Rhea hid her baby son Zeus in a cave to save him from his father Uranus, who had swallowed all her previous children like so many oysters. (It had been prophesied that one of his children would kill him, and he was determined to frustrate the prediction.) But there in his cave the young sun-god was secretly nursed with his foster-brother Pan by the *she-goat* Amalthea, who nourished them with her milk, while the daughters of Melisseus fed them with *honey*. (Melisseus means honey.) Zeus, grateful for Amalthea's services, later set her among the stars as Capricorn. He also borrowed one of her horns and gave it to Melissius' daughters, where it became the Cornucopia of Plenty, which gave its fortunate owner whatever he most desired to eat and drink. It sounds like a forerunner of the Grail, which also had this magical capacity. Can it be said that the Grail is stored in Capricorn's horn - the rich store of his inherited wisdom? This magical vessel is concealed in more than one of these Zodiac signs.

But it is time to press on, like the climbing goat, to Aquarius, the Hill of Syon, at Osterley.

Aquarius

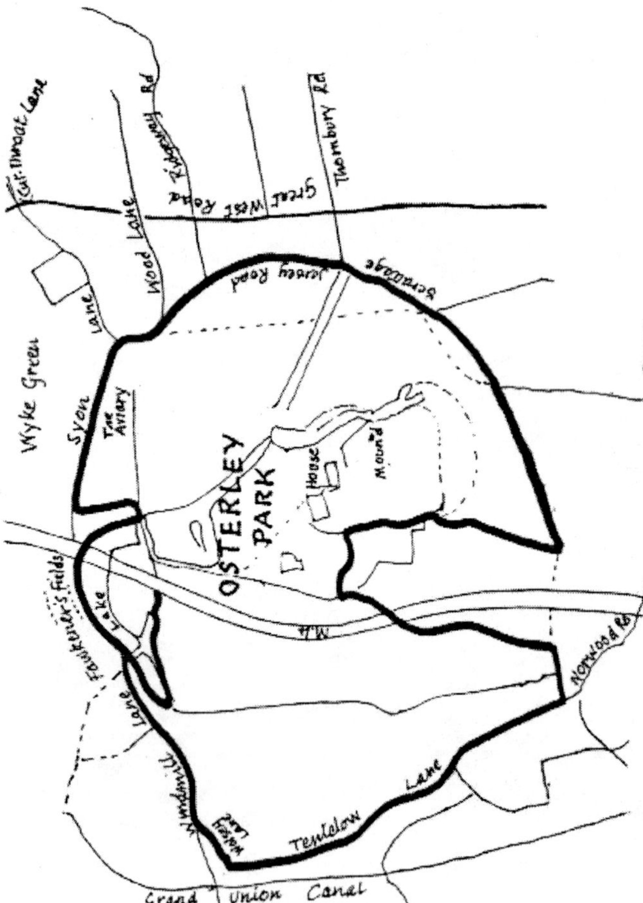

Cut-Throat Lane
Ridgeway Rd
Thornbury Rd
Great West Road
Wood Lane
Jersey Road
Scrattage
Lane
Wyke Green
Syon
The Aviary
OSTERLEY PARK
House
Mound
M4
Lake
Faulkener's Fields
Lane
Windmill
Tentelow
Lane
Norwood Rd
Grand Union Canal

Aquarius

Osterley's rounded Park can equally be read as Phoenix-eagle - or as Waterpot, Cauldron or Grail.

The earliest Chaldean sign for Aquarius was simply a water-pot. But crested bird, Cauldron and Grail all symbolise much the same idea; rebirth on a higher octave. Crested eagles, phoenixes even peacocks sometimes appeared on Roman and early Christian tombstones; the crest signifying where the spirit escaped from the body. Just as the old or dead were plunged into the legendary cauldron and were revived, so the phoenix rose from its own ashes with the new year. Some see Aquarius as a sort of Davey escape hatch from the wheel of reincarnation on earth - but this could only apply in human terms to those initiates who have mastered the many lessons of previous lives.

Although today the winter solstice occurs on the cusp of Sagittarius/Capricorn, due to the precession of the equinoxes, some 2000 years ago it was on the cusp of Capricorn/Aquarius - which accounts for this symbolism.

Ancient Greeks identified Aquarius with Ganymede, the beautiful youth who was snatched from Mount Ida's peak by Zeus in the form of an eagle, to make him cup-bearer to the gods on Olympus. *Was this tale inspired by the cup-winged eagle of terrestrial Zodiacs?* But when they added the Waterman as a fourth human figure to the Zodiac they unwittingly corrupted its original three human signs; its family Trinity of Sagittarian Sun-god, Virgoan Earth-Mother and Geminian Son(s). (The two sons signify our divided nature, being destined to become one.) This earlier configuration of only three human signs, seen now in terrestrial Zodiacs alone, has thus been lost. But it is nonetheless of great significance, being one of the factors that point to the Zodiac as ancestor of all ancient religions.

Ganymede in the Mysteries was not just a pretty face; he typified the perfected Man, who, the ancients taught, could fly free from the earthly school of recurring lives, being drawn irresistibly sunwards, from whence he could help irradiate the whole solar system. When needed, such spirits could return to earth if they chose, to enlighten those still in semi-darkness below.. That such ideas were taught by the Druids is apparent in sundry old poems, according to the Welsh scholar Edward Davies, who also gives an old Breton legend in his "*Celtic Researches*" of 1809 which points much the same way.

In this tale the young son of the Prince de Pol de Leon dies in a cave by the sea on the knees of the great Goddess of Nature whose belt is the Zodiac. Zephyrs waft him aloft through the clouds, which he sees are formed of the souls of men and beasts who are too wedded to earthly desires to rise higher. Howling in the wind, they seek any opportunity to return to earth by entering into any recently generated body, animal or human, that corresponds to their lowly spiritual state. The prince next rises to the moon, where he sees souls in a state of forgetfulness in a sea of ice. When an eclipse forms a long dark tunnel to earth, numbers of these descend along it to resume their round of lives on earth once more. But our prince is made of finer stuff, and at last approaches the sun, at first with dread, but with increasing joy as he perceives that it is formed by vibrant souls floating in a sea of bliss. These are the sages, the friends of mankind. They, when thrice purified in the sun's crucible, can ascend to still higher worlds from which there is no return. Davies remarks that this concept is not Christian, and is probably Druidic.

In later Arthurian legend, Perceval and Galahad his ideal echo something of the same tale, sailing to Sarras among the stars to achieve the Grail in Solomon's ship - the ship of Sol the sun. Galahad the perfected man did not return; Perceval came back to enlighten those on earth... The sun-god Zeus himself bore Ganymede heavenwards, from whence as Water-Carrier he can pour something of his vitality back to earth.

Zodiac pilgrims will rejoice to see two great stone eagles on either side of the imposing steps leading up to the great house. Indeed, birds predominated here, for Osterley was once famous for the rare feathered fowl in its aviary. A subconscious tribute to its Phoenix, flying overall? The Aquarian birds of both Zodiacs are literally Water-Carriers, for Glastonbury's Eagle/Phoenix grasps famous Chalice Well in its beak on Glastonbury Tor, while Osterley's eagle head and beak are formed by a lakein the park.. The vanished village of *Scrattage* on one wing (now Jersey Road) seems to remember its sharp talons. Its crest was at Fawkener's Fields, now a golf course. Thereby hangs a legend.

The tale goes that Edward III gave Osterley to a man called Fawkener on condition that he rode round it annually with a falcon on his wrist. Why this strange condition? Did Edward, a great Arthurian, know the Zodiac secret of this eagle-Phoenix at Osterley, and endeavouring to perpetuate it, give the hill to Fawkener because he had the right name? Or did the odd condition of ownership earn him his name? The fact, whichever way it was, is one of those strange coincidences with which Zodiac pilgrims are by now familiar, and the name Fawkener's Fields still exists to make us wonder..

When Henry V's Brigittine monastery of Syon at Twickenham was moved (by some Zodiacal magic) to the site of the present Syon House, its land included Osterley, which finally equated it with Glastonbury's "New Jerusalem". And though its hill can hardly compete with the dramatic Tor, it too became an

Glastonbury Tor

Aquarian hill of Zion. In the grounds there is a mound, and though now slightingly known as an 18th. century "ice-box" , I can't help wondering whether it is not much older. Did Brigit's perpetual fires once keep this ice-box warm? Brigit after all is remembered at Glastonbury, and is pictured on the Tor's tower.

Capricorn noses Osterley's hill at Wyke Green, just as Glastonbury's goat noses the base of the Tor at Wick. Coincidence again? I think not. Place-name dictionaries explain such names as marshy, dairy-farming land, but I suspect that originally the opposite was the case. Wicks, Wykes and Weekes still name holy hills, as at Malvern Wych, or Wyke high above Weymouth and Winchester, or Newton Abbot's High Weeke. Brigit' s candle*wick* or beacon-fire lighting the seven-terraced Tor shows Capricorn the seven steps to illumination. The seven days of the week, like the Chaldean planet-tiered Ziggurats, are meant to be daily steps nearer heaven. Is it accident merely, that there are twenty-one steps (three sevens) in the ascent to Osterley House?

The old Canaanite festival of Weeks adopted by the Jews (forty-nine days or seven weeks) led early Christians to the illumination of Pentecost (which means the fiftieth day) - or *Whit*sun. Such hills, whether natural or artificial, were Whit- or inspirational mounds from which bardic law, poetry and prophecy were proclaimed. Moses received the Ten Commandments, Christ preached his sermon on such a mount. Prehistoric Merlin's Mount at Marlborough College still whispers its Druidic seven-tiered message. Like its colossal neighbour Silbury Hill at Avebury, it must also have been a ley-mound marking the course of the old Bath Road. These "tons" - literally tons of earth - were centres for Eisteddfods, schooling, law-giving, markets and fairs, thus "tons" became " towns" . Our oldest law-courts, schools and universities lie beneath such mounds, and where they existed, Norman barons built their motte-and-bailey castles on them, thus commanding (and frequently suppressing) the centres of religion, free speech, law, education and commerce. Similarly, the word "motte," old French for a hill or mound, has slipped downhill since, to be submerged in the moat below; but one can discern its earlier meaning in the word "moot" or meeting place. For few without a swimsuit would want to meet in a moat. Much the same down-shifting seems to have happened to the word Wick. I suspect too that the recurring name Whitchurch (whose churches were seldom white even when new) indicates a church built on a prehistoric holy hill.

Was Dick *Whit*tington inspired to interpret the church bells' octave on Highgate's Druidic Whit-mound of free speech, *Parliament* Hill? Did he experience on its summit the mighty rushing wind of Whit, wisdom and prophecy that rewards the visionary climber? On such mounds the eighth step (*huit*) doubles the first step's vibrations, thus beginning a new octave, a life transfigured; the spectrum whirls into *whit*e, and the initiate becomes the Master, "his garments so white no fuller could whiten them." Another such holy hill is at Harrow, crowned with a church like Glastonbury Tor, but being seven miles north of Osterley, we can hardly claim it for our Zodiac. However, its early name was "Hearg" - Heathen Temple. And its Norman legend seems to imply a maze, like that on the Tor. A thief they say stole a monstrance from its church, but apparently overcome with guilt, wandered bemused in circles round the hill until he was caught. Was Harrow Hill once a seven-tiered Ziggurat? Those who thread mazes know that only the outermost rings lead to the centre; when you are furthest out you are nearest home. So it is with Capricorn. He has left Kew Garden's heaven for Brentford's man-made hell, but Syon House's heavenly gates (particularly pearly when viewed from the river) are there to admit him to Osterley's Easter Resurrection. Three adjacent signs here stamp Man's evolutionary journey on the landscape - from primal innocence through bitter experience to final illumination.

Sir Thomas Gresham built the first grand house at Osterley in Tudor times. His stables and the two towers on each end of the house are all that remain now of that period. An able financier, he acquired great wealth, and built London's first Royal Exchange - to the lasting benefit of the country's economy. Aquarius can be a great reformer and benefactor. He also founded Gresham College, to help educate Londoners. Though he infuriated the locals at the time by fencing in an area of Hounslow Heath some six miles round Osterley, he has earned our undying gratitude today, like Charles I's equally unpopular enclosure of Richmond Park. For without these unintentional benefactions undoubtedly both vast open spaces would by now be entirely built over.

The history of Osterley certainly echoes the character of its sign. Aquarius denotes the rise of the Common Man; and though Gresham was not as common as all that (his father was a Norfolk knight), it can well be imagined that the dukes and earls of neighbouring Syon looked down their aristocratic noses at this wealthy parvenu. Gresham was entrusted with keeping poor Lady Mary Grey under lock and key - a curious echo from Syon's unhappy past. Mary, sister of Lady Jane Grey, seeing Jane's unhappy fate for marrying too high, decided for safety's sake to secretly marry a *commoner,* the Royal Sergeant-Porter Thomas Keyes - (an ominous name as it turned out.) But this incurred Elizabeth's wrath. She separated the pair at once, putting Keyes under lock and key in the Fleet, and imprisoning Mary at Osterley. She was only freed seven years later, when her husband had died in prison. Poor ill-fated sisters! Mary, heart-broken, died soon afterwards. This tug-of-war between commoners and nobles recurs, as we shall see, in the history of Osterley on Aquarius, the sign of the common man.

Another early and even lowlier owner was the son of the Puritan preacher Praise-God-Barebones. Dropping the e's from Barebones he became Nicholas Barbon, and made a fortune rebuilding London after the great fire of 1666. He cashed in on the public's fear of another conflagration and made a second fortune selling fire insurance. Capricornian Barebones resurrects as the Osterley Phoenix!

The next owner was also of lowly origins. Francis Child from Wiltshire was apprenticed at the age of fourteen to a London goldsmith and by shrewd application to business became rich enough to found Child's bank. He married an untitled heiress, became richer than ever, and like Dick Whittington was made Lord Mayor of London - and knighted.

It was his grandson Francis who asked Robert Adam to create the splendid Georgian mansion that we can all visit today. Adam, who had created such elegance at Syon, was perhaps fired by Osterley's competitive spirit, and exceeded himself. But before young Francis could enjoy these splendours he died aged 27 on the very eve of his marriage. Aquarius is ruled by Uranus, and this seems to be one of its lightning-strikes. The building was completed by Francis' brother Robert Child, now head of the bank.

Walpole of Gothick Strawberry Hill went to see it and commented "Oh, the palace of palaces! And yet a palace *sans* crown, *sans* coronet, but such expense! Such taste! Such profusion! The old house I have often seen, which was built by Sir Thomas Gresham; but it is so improved and enriched that all the Percies and Seymours of Syon must die of envy." In emphasising the new democratic rivalry of Osterley with the old aristocracy next door, Walpole had hit on the essentially Aquarian character of the place. He was less enchanted with the park, in fact stigmatising it as the "ugliest spot in the universe." This opinion will not be shared by visitors today, for its lakes are lovely, and its cedars have had time since Walpole's day to grow to truly magnificent proportions, and are now not least among the wonders of the place.

Robert Child had no son to perpetuate his name and succeed as head of his bank - and his daughter fell in love with the handsome young Earl of Westmoreland. Most men in Child's position would have been delighted at this titled catch, but (it could only happen under Aquarius) her father angrily forbade the match. He was anxious to perpetuate his name,;but could could hardly expect the earl to forego his title and agree to take the name of Child. Worse, the Earls of Westmoreland were connected to the Percies of Northumberland and Syon. Too much!

The cunning young suitor asked him at dinner one night "What would you do if you were in love with a girl and her father refused his consent?" "Why, run away with her, to be sure!" was his unguarded reply. So without delay the couple eloped by coach to Gretna Green - hotly pursued by the banker, furious that he had been trapped, and mounted, with his servants, on fast horses. Uranus gives sudden inspiration and changes of fortune. What could be more inspirational than the suitor's question, or more Uranian than a bolt to Gretna Green?).

But at Baldock the couple's coach was nearly overtaken, and "Rapid" Westmoreland as he was called, obviously a man of quick Uranian decisions, shot the leading pursuer's horse dead under him. The other servants stopped in their tracks - and Robert Child realising that more bloodshed might endanger his daughter, called off the chase, and could only consent to the marriage. It seems he was broken-hearted, for he died shortly afterwards, having cut his daughter out of his will. (A very substantial Aquarian reversal of fortune!) Robert Child's widow later married Lord Ducie - (the pressure of a title was unrelenting) - which must have made the banker turn in his grave. By another strange Zodiacal coincidence, his granddaughter died of a burning fever in Dublin's *Phoenix* Park.

This grand-daughter Sarah, to whom the Child fortune was bequeathed in the hope that the name would continue, married the 5th. Earl of Jersey. So titles won in the end, despite Robert Child's determination - at least until the 20th. century, when the grand house and park became public property opened to us all for a small fee, so that we the commons, can visit it and wonder at its magnificence. So perhaps the Childs won, after all?

But the Zodiac saga is not yet finished - for Lady Adele Villiers, like her grandmother, also eloped from Osterley to Gretna Green - but this time to marry a *commoner*. The Dowager countess is said to have remarked, on seeing the gallant captain of the heiress' choice, that she had no idea the middle classes were so clean! (I am indebted to Cecil Roberts' book "And so to Bath" for these fascinating Osterley details.)

But there is more. The bishop of Raphoe, father of a Regency Countess of Jersey at Osterley, liked to play highwayman. He would see that dinner-guest's pistols were left at the entrance when they arrived and secretly unloaded while they dined - then masked, would hold them up on Hounslow Heath as they returned home. But one guest, forewarned, insisted on keeping his loaded firearm with him, and shot the predatory prelate when he was told to stand and deliver. Some accounts say it was a fatal wound - others merely that the bishop was mysteriously unfit for services for some weeks. Can anything more Uranian be conceived than this preposterous tale? For Uranus not only gives shocks, but also tends towards unorthodox views on religion. It is hardly a recommendation of the state of the Church of England at this time.

But Uranus had not finished with Osterley. The planet's last strike was in 1949 - and a devastating one at that. The famous Osterley collection of paintings, one of the most distinguished in the country, containing work by Joshua Reynolds, Van Dyck, Poussin, Claude Lorraine, Lawrence and

Romney, was to be kept at Osterley when the 9th.earl of Jersey, strapped for cash, gave the house and its invaluable contents to the National Trust. But interminable negotiations over the cost of maintaining these treasures irritated him so much that he decided to keep the pictures. And when he removed them to a warehouse while building a suitable gallery for them in Jersey, his retreat from Osterley's encroaching suburbia, the warehouse caught fire and all the precious paintings were burnt to a cinder. So perished one of our greatest picture collections. But at least some portraits have been reproduced in the National Trust book on sale at Osterley, so that we can see in miniature what some of its dramatis personae looked like. Alas, the highwayman-bishop is not among them..

It would be delightful to be able to say that the astronomer William Herschel discovered Uranus here. But in fact he *did* find it at Slough, only a few miles west along the Bath Road. George III went to see his giant forty-foot telescope while it was in the making, and walked with his family and the Archbishop of Canterbury through its huge barrel while it lay on the ground. Taking the prelate by the hand to help him, he said “Come my lord Bishop, I will show you the way to Heaven!”

There is another tale of George III which not only shows his good nature but the essentially independent character of Osterley. The king, returning from hunting, attempted to pass through Wyke Farm on the edge of Osterley park on his way home to Kew, but found the gate locked. He called to a man nearby to open it , but the fellow merely replied “Nay, ye maun gang aboot. “Open the gate at once! I'm the king!” “Why, may be; but ye maun gang aboot, for all that”, was the surly reply. So the king had to ride round nearly the whole enclosure of Osterley to get home. The farmer, who was away at the time, heard of this encounter on his return, and fearing serious royal reprisals hastened to Kew to apologise for his tenant's intransigence. The king, who was himself called Farmer George for his simple style of living, received him at once without ceremony and merely said "I wish I had such fine honest fellows in my pay as your old Gang-Aboot. Tell him I like his honesty, and shall be glad to see him here some day." And in fact the independent labourer actually went to see the king at Kew. No doubt he got a better reception than he gave; one hopes his manners improved for the occasion.

Osterley seems to have echoes in another intriguing place along the Bath Road three or four miles west of Aquarius at Colnbrook, where the ancient Ostrich Inn is a hostelry Zodiac pilgrims should not miss. It boasts a real stuffed ostrich, and you can read a copy of Magna Carta there while you drink. It also has two significant legends. Dick Turpin is said to have leapt from its upper window onto Black Bess's back and galloped north to York and freedom just as Bow Street Runners raced upstairs to arrest him - an escape reminiscent of Osterley's flights to Gretna green.

The other legend is older and more sinister. The couple who kept the inn were called Jarman, and used to lock guests' valuables in their safe, ostensibly to keep them from robbers, then while the guest slept, would unbolt the floor beneath his bed - tipping him into a bath of boiling water in the kitchen below. They would then take the body at night and throw it in the river Colne nearby, so it would appear to have drowned. A wealthy traveller, Thomas Cole, stayed at the Ostrich, and perturbed by a premonition of impending evil, ordered musicians to come and play to raise his spirits. He was right to be depressed, for he was to be the infamous couple's next victim. Next morning his horse was found wandering, and the Jarmans were suspected of foul play. They fled into Windsor forest but were caught - and confessed to sixty such murders.

The name Jarman - could it mean *Water-Jarman?* The sixty murders, the minutes of the Zodiac clock? The Ostrich was founded in 1106 by the Templars as a hospice on the Bath road "for the good of travellers in this world and their salvation in the next" - as its charter mysteriously states. Could the Templars have spread this tale as a subtle intimation of the Cauldron of Aquarius, a few miles east along the road? Whether they did or not, it is a strange Zodiacal coincidence. And Thomas Cole - could he be Old King Cole, calling for his fiddlers three, and could the bowl he asked for in old age be the rejuvenating Aquarian Cauldron?

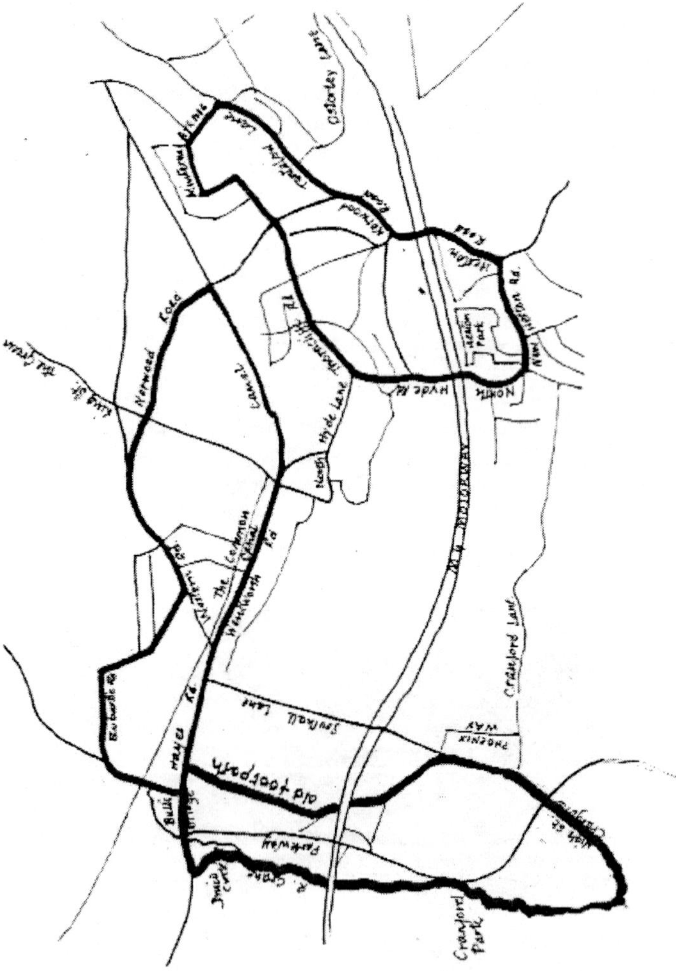
Norwood Road
Hyde Lane
North Hyde Lane
North Hyde Rd
Heston Road
New Heston Rd.
Heston Park
Osterley Lane
Tentelow Lane
Wentworth Rd
The Common
Hayes Rd
Southall Lane
Phoenix Way
Cranford Lane
old footpath
Parkway
R. Crane
Cranford Park
M4 Motorway

Pisces

Pisces

Fish are weighed by the cran - or used to be - so it is tempting to search for one of this Zodiac pair in the river Crane at Cranford. The other is just west of Osterley, at Heston. (North Hyde Road draws another fish, but as it is too small I have thrown it back. And the third fish in the diagram is really too modern to include, for its underside is drawn by Grand Union Canal.)

However, the name North *Hyde* could be significant at this Zodiac's northern point, for it echoes the 12 *Hides* of land given to Joseph of Arimathea to maintain him and his followers when he landed at Wearyall Hill on the Glastonbury Zodiac's northern Fish. For these Hides, said Mrs. Maltwood, were at once the twelve "animal-hides" or hidden figures, and a land measurement. It is the strangest Zodiacal coincidence that Joseph should be remembered as landing there, for he brought Christianity with the Grail to Britain, and the Fishes were its earliest sign in the catacombs, long before the cross was adopted.

It seems he knew where to land; or if his story is only legend, at least his legend-maker knew. For he is said to have planted his staff on Wearyall Hill, where it sprouted and ever after has magically flowered both at Christmas and Easter. Cuttings from it in Glastonbury Abbey grounds also flower at these times - and aptly enough, botanists have identified it as a Mediterranean thorn. Some see this thorn as a calendar-peg, planted on Pisces' hill at the time when the old Druidic dispensation was being decimated by the Roman invasion, to signify on this clock of ages the beginning of the Piscean Age, when the new religion was grafted on the old.

For the thorn before Christianity was sacred to the goddess of the British Mysteries.

Joseph is cited as ancestor of the mysterious line of Fisher-kings of the Grail Castle in Arthurian legend, thus connecting Glastonbury's main legends together. There is nothing more mystical in our Island story than this tale of Joseph's coming (some say with his nephew Jesus,) - and they centre on Glastonbury'Fisher's Hill - on Pisces, the poet and mystic of the Zodiac..

Brons, one of Joseph's company, is said to have caught a mystical fish, which when eaten revitalised those Grail initiates who partook of it. For this single achievement he was thenceforth called the Great Fisher. But this title and ritual meal can be traced back to Middle Eastern Mysteries, even earlier than the fish breakfast cooked for his disciples by the risen Christ on Galilee's shore. It also echoes the Celtic Salmon of Wisdom, which inspired the man who merely touched its scales and sucked his thumb. The fish, apparently so chaste, has long signified baptism to new life - and all life begins in water.

Can the old Hundred of Elthorne, which includes both the Kingston Zodiac Fishes, and Thornbury nearby, be an echo of Joseph's thorn? Elthorne's early name, *Hele*-torne, hints at even more ancient solar ritual. Exploring the Cranford Fish where Watersplash Lane meets the Crane, I found a small ramparted circle surrounded by hawthorns. They were flowering, for it was Mayday, and host to hordes of Red Admiral butterflies.. A Druid grove in industrial Middlesex? Even a derelict car rusting in the grass beside me only added spice to the strange delight that comes of finding Paradise in rubbish dumps. Heaven is where you're at, these Zodiacs seem to say; turn a derelict stone and start an angel's wing. Since then roaring new Parkway has been extended northwards, and I was unable to find this little circle on my last visit. Has it fallen victim to the new dual carriageway? On the earlier occasion I was certainly under Neptune's spell, despite all the 20th. century could do, with its new Parkway and M4 motorway, its ponderous flying fish from Heath Row thundering overhead, cutting rudely across the Red Admirals' bows..

It must be said that the water-signs in the Kingston Zodiac all proved the most elusive to find; but as I have Scorpio rising and the moon in Pisces, this may have to do with the pilgrim's difficulties in finding ones-self. Someone with a different horoscope may be able to see them at once - so I am open to correction in these areas.

(I have already confessed that I couldn't find the effigy of my own sun-sign, Libra, until a scornful student pointed out the bird-form, using the main roads of Kingston with no problem at all.) So I can only regard these blanks of perception as personally significant...

Though the Piscean area in the Kingston Zodiac can hardly compete with Glastonbury either with legends or the clarity of its effigies, it is not without some teasing clues. As far back as 800 AD the Mercian king Offa gave some land at Hayes to the Archbishop of Canterbury. Did he know that it was the "North Hyde" of the Kingston Zodiac, and want to sanctify it? At any rate Archbishops had a manor here for many centuries, and the ancient parish church of St Mary's in its vast churchyard still reflects this glory. John Betjeman has described this church at Hayes as one of the chief gems of Middlesex, and it is certainly worth seeing, if only for its huge mediaeval mural of St Christopher, struggling with the Christ-child through the waves - a rare treasure. Zodiac pilgrims will rejoice as I did, to see the *fishes* (and even a mermaid) disporting about his feet.

What more could one ask? But for antiquarians there are many other things to see here; an old lych-gate, a splendid pillared Norman font, a barrel-vaulted roof and several early brasses. The Archbishop's old Manor is still there, though it has lost its once-splendid gateway, and is now an Old Peoples' home. Though Hayes is hardly the most romantic spot to visit today, its old village pond which once reflected the church now filled in, and much of the place a byword for industrial development - there is a peculiarly nostalgic thrill in finding such vestigial traces of departed beauty and history in 20th century suburban sprawl. Bishop Stigand who crowned King Harold, must have been here, also Lanfranc, Anselm and Thomas a Becket. But to see this wonderful old church one must visit at service times, for it is not otherwise kept open.

The map hints at three or four possible fish in the area where they ought to be, but mostly relying for their outlines on historically recent canals, or worse, railways. The river Crane is at least ancient, and by its name a great fish finder! But it was the river's Saxon name, *Fish*bourne, which occurs in Offa's charter of 790, that helped me to outline the westernmost Piscean effigy.

Pisces the mystic has a tendency to retire from life; celibacy comes more easily to natives of this sign than to any other. And suitably enough there was a monastery at Harmondsworth, just north of Heathrow. But though its buildings disappeared after the Dissolution, its magnificent tithe barn, one of the largest in the country, is still there to be visited. It is one of the little-known wonders of Middlesex, and thankfully is now preserved by English Heritage. Glastonbury, that mystical centre between Pisces and Aquarius on the Somerset Zodiac, has its great abbey ruins, and Zodiac pilgrims may be forgiven for seeing this awe-inspiring barn as a cathedral too, with its 13 threshing bays and huge oak hammer-beams from Windsor Forest. And while there don't fail to see the church's Norman door.

Harmondsworth village itself has Piscean qualities; hidden and secluded as it is, so near the busy Bath Road and the even busier mayhem of London Airport, it keeps its charm unchanged, as if it didn't quite belong in the present century at all.

Another church bordering this sign with strangely Piscean clues is at Harlington. Its splendid Norman doorway, deemed the finest in Middlesex, is ornamented with cats' heads, their long tongues lolling out. (Are they salivating at the thought of Cranford's Fish?) But what really dumbfounded me was to see in the chancel the oddest statue of St Peter the fisherman, with a *fish* keeping his place in the bible he holds. This strange conceit was one suspects made deliberately by a parson with the apt name of *Haddock*,who did much to restore the church, and even had the grace to die on All Souls' Day, as his commemorative tablet records. (All Soles Day? Perish the thought). There is a stained-glass window of St. Christopher battling with the waves here as well, to continue the watery theme.

More Haddock graves in the churchyard seem designed to make certain we don't miss which sign we are on, as we walk down its noble avenue of Cypresses. There is also a gaunt cedar with a legend that it grew from seed brought by a crusader from the Holy Land. Can it really be so old? Another of Harlington' antiquities, its famous churchyard yew, still sprouting indomitably from its 1000-year-old stump, somehow makes the story easier to believe. Lebanon cedars were used in building Solomon's Temple, for besides being resinous and thus durable wood, the Tree of Life of the eastern Cabala was coniferous. Its cones, opening to the sun, represented that inspirational gland, the *pine*al; ancient sculptures show Assyrian priests lustrating the Tree of Life with it. The Templars, guardians of the Grail and active in Jerusalem and the Holy Land, learnt to see the Mysteries of East and West as one. Surely it was a crusading Templar who planted

Harlington's cedar-Tree of Life at this north-west gate of the Kingston Zodiac? Strangely enough, the Earl of Harlington dropped his H's to become one of Charles II's secret Cabal, which consisted of Clifford, Arlington, Buckingham, Ashley-Cooper and Lauderdale.

The Pisces area in this Zodiac is devoid of great houses - in sharp contrast to Osterley, Syon, Gunnersbury and Chiswick House which still adorn the previous two signs. But they are on the zenith of the Zodiac representing the rewards of long endeavour and success in careers. Astrologically, Pisces begins a retreat from worldly glory; its key-words are dissolution, disillusion, seclusion. Neptune its ruler with its numinous ray leads the native on to higher things like art, poetry, mysticism - which seldom pay in terms of earthly rewards. So Cranford, once a seat of the Earls of Berkeley at Cranford, has been allowed to fall down when the family retreated before the rising tide of suburbia. But at least the Park has been kept, while the grand stables are still there - a reminder of departed glory, when the Berkeley coach-and-six rattled up to London in great style. Hemmed in between Heathrow with its unending shoals of flying fish, the dual carriageway of Parkway and the roaring- M4, its present state is a reminder that Pisces is the sign of self-imprisonment. Indeed, the undistinguished architecture of the whole area emphasises the low profile sought by Pisceans. Gypsies are now encamped on the edge of Cranford Park, showing another aspect of natives of this dual sign. When they are not sheltering in an institution, they are inveterate wanderers. The M4, though it slices through the two effigies as if they were on a fishmonger's slab, gives them an alluring gateway to the West, and from Heathrow they can fly away in all directions..

The church in Cranford Park, now crouching beneath the M4 motorway, is rebuilt on Saxon foundations which were probably the work of the ubiquitous St Dunstan, to whom it is dedicated. Tiny though it is, it is crammed with monuments.

More than half-a-dozen 17th century effigies of the Aston family, almost life-size, crowd the little chancel - not recumbent but kneeling and brightly painted as if they were still alive. Such a group, surely unique anywhere, must make today's worshippers, competing for space at the altar rail, wonder at the thin line between life and death - a truly Piscean preoccupation. For Pisces is the last sign of the Zodiac, where life dissolves and prepares to begin again. And many memorials to the Berkeleys, including a superb reclining marble of the first Lady Berkeley to live here -an effigy of unusual beauty - help to make this rich little church a visit not to be missed.

When the rip-roaring Earls of Berkeley were here, though as an ancient and notable family under the influence of Jupiter, Pisces' co-ruler, they seemed occasionally to fall under Pisces' watery influence. They would hunt over the glass cloches of Cranford's nursery gardens with scant regard for their tenants' livelihood, or their horses' fetlocks, as if they were splashing through waves on the foreshore of a glassy sea. Grantley Berkeley once chased a stag all the way to the steps of the British Museum. And between these sportive forays, this same Grantley wrote poetry, passionately proclaiming his love of the countryside.

An 18th century Berkeley earl took for his mistress one of three alluring daughters of a butcher in Bath and had four sons by her before considering that their illegitimacy precluded any of them from inheriting his title. When he eventually realised this, he pretended that he had married her before any of them were born, but that the parson had destroyed the register.

Friendly with George IV, he hoped to get away with it, but the ensuing trial provoked such scandal that even that licentious monarch withdrew his favour. So the earl belatedly married his long-suffering mistress, insisting to the last that it was a repeat performance. Pisces is not above a little deception (a negative misuse of Neptune's ray) when its suits his purpose.

Morton, the fifth (and first legitimate) son, resolutely refused to take his title when offered it on his father's death, saying with truly Piscean self-sacrifice that to do so would dishonour his parents. So the earldom lapsed, and he lived thereafter in a small house on the estate as plain Morton Berkeley - and was much loved locally for his humility.

But his mother, the mistress/countess, was never sure that she would not be arrested for being party to her husband's deception, even after his death. So she built a tunnel from her house to the outside wall, with a coach always ready for flight abroad, in case the worst should happen. She need not have worried as it turned out; being a woman of great character and charm, quite capable of fulfilling her high position and sympathetic to all, whether high or low, so her popularity left her untroubled by the law. This typical Piscean charm seems to be a wise precaution of Evolution for the children of Neptune, often so helpless in the hard world. For where would they be without patrons and helpers? Interestingly, she displayed another Piscean trait; she is recorded as filling her wine-glass to the very brim, and raising it to her lips without spilling a drop, saying “None of my sons could do this!”

There were other Piscean eccentricities. An 18th century Berkeley admiral who lived there in retirement had verandas built on to the house to resemble the poops of the old warships of his time, from which he would sweep the landscape with his telescope as if he were still at sea. (These can be seen in a photo of the vanished house on the west wall of the church). His chaplain, obviously under the same Neptunian ray, invented a land-yacht on wheels, on which he would scud through the park whenever there was enough wind to fill his sails, as if he were at sea..

One of the most interesting old buildings still extant in this area is an inn at Heston, the old Queens' Head. Now called the Hungry Horse in the regrettable fashion for witty pub-names, it is an imperative visit for Zodiac pilgrims, for it will inspire them with some of the out-of this-world amazement induced by Harmondsworth barn. Old oak beams everywhere, its barn-like roof with brightly painted gesso mouldings dating from Tudor times, its busts of queens of England from Boadicea onward adorning stone niches, and a suit of mediaeval armour are among the intriguing wonders to catch your eye as you drink your pint. But remember as you imbibe that both Neptune and Jupiter can lead to excess. Neptune can also bewilder, so don't try to follow the old sign-posts collected here - for they point every-which-way as if to confuse Pisces, the bemused wanderer. The Fishes are in evidence here too, darting about in a pond that extends - preposterously - underneath part of this old inn.

Heston church is undistinguished except for its old lych-gate, which dates from 1450 and still has the wooden pulley-wheel for raising coffins. But on the north side of the churchyard is a white gravestone that tells a truly Piscean tale. It commemorates poor Frederick White, whose sufferings brought to an end the long-established system of flogging, both in the army and the navy. A private soldier liable to brain-storms, he struck an officer when unbearably provoked, and was flogged so badly that he died soon afterwards. Up to a thousand lashes were sometimes administered in these inhuman punishments, and deaths were by no means uncommon. But he must have been popular, for his fellow-privates in Hounslow Barracks became so mutinous that the officer responsible (oddly enough, a Captain Whyte) feared for his life and had to take their musket-balls from them. Rumours of the tragedy leaked out, and came to the compassionate ear of the vicar of Heston. So when he was asked to bury the body he refused until a post-mortem was arranged. The army did all they could to prevent this, but to the undying credit of the vicar he saw that it took place despite them, and descriptions of the hideously flayed body were reported in news-sheets. Such a public outcry followed that eventually Parliament was forced to ban the cruel custom - one that had for centuries gone unquestioned.

Is it not interesting that the first protest began in sensitive and sympathetic Pisces? Private White's was an involuntary service to humanity, but the fact remains that Pisces, the last sign of the Zodiac, is astrologically the sign of self-sacrifice for others. And though he died in Hounslow's militant Aries, it seems right that he should be buried and remembered in Pisces. One more point. The recurring name of White, so reminiscent of fish, is surely strange; it seems there were *two* white fish involved...

There was another great house near Harlington, though somewhat north of the sign - Dawley Farm. Lord Bolingbroke enlarged the original building to make a country retreat (significantly, he called it his *hermitage*) where he entertained the literati of the day, and as these included Alexander Pope, Dryden, Gay and Voltaire, it became a real poet's corner, worthy of mention in this chapter on Pisces, the poet of the Zodiac. Here Dean Swift read Gulliver's Travels to the assembled company, an apt choice for Pisces the Wanderer. Now like the Berkeleys' house at Cranford, the mansion has disappeared, leaving only an interminable wall enclosing the estate. On this flat land an artificial hill has been built, from which one can see to the North Downs, Windsor Castle, and across London to Canary Wharf. One *should* be able to obtain a view from mystical Pisces; Glastonbury's Wearyall Hill gives a splendid one. The fact that Dawley's hill is artificial and recent only demonstrates to me that the sign's influence is still potent here. And to prove the point, in Stockley Park's new leisure centre, recently built in the south of the Dawley estate, is a lake with a circle of sculptured swimmers, submerged just below the water except for their elegant legs -

which rise vertically, toes pointing skywards. Did the sculptor know he was so near Pisces, who in astrology rules the feet?

The Piscean area is well watered by small streams, once notable for their fishing. The general water-level is only a few feet underground, so wells are easily sunk, and the land very fertile. Heston corn was so good that Queen Elizabeth insisted on having her bread made from its mill. Nursery gardens to feed London were numerous, and itinerant workers came from far afield to harvest the crops, living nomadically in tents, Piscean style. It was this seasonal invasion combined with constant traffic along the Bath Road that brought Colnbrook's Court of Pie-Powder into being. Its intriguing name comes from the French “pied poudreux” - dusty feet. Those Piscean feet again!

So choking was the summer dust here that it threatened the success of Beau Brummel's fashionable Bath season, so he had pumps erected along the road to allay it, worked by liveried attendants when coaches came by. Two of these are still there on the left of the old Bath road, where it parts from the newer Colnbrook bypass.In winter however, the road became a quagmire; the going was said to be “good” when coach-wheels only sank two feet into the mud.. The name of nearby Slough says it all.

On Slough's Salt Hill, by the way, is the ancient barrow-mound called Eton Montem, long the scene of college festivities. Whether it was once Sol Hill, one of those mounds of the sun-worshipping Druids, from whose height poetry and law were proclaimed, and beneath which some of our oldest schools were founded - or whether the hill above Eton was Windsor itself, is uncertain. But Eton Montem was for centuries the scene of great annual celebrations, not only for the schoolboys, but for all their friends and relations too. It is a small antiquity not to be missed, especially valuable in such an unattractive blot on the 20th century landscape as Slough.

We have strayed far from Pisces, but having come as far as Colnbrook it is tempting to visit Horton, only a mile further - for here the youthful Milton lived. (Who knows how far the waves of Pisces' influence can ripple?) Here he lost both his mother and friend in one year, and his resulting elegy "Lycidas", commemorating young Edward King who drowned in the Irish Sea, is surely Piscean

"Weep no more, shepherds, weep no more
For Lycidas your sorrow is not dead.
Sunk though he be beneath the watery floor
So sinks the day-star in the ocean bed..."

"Il Penseroso" also breathes a melancholy that is typical of Pisces the Poet. And though Milton tried to cheer himself up in "L' Allegro" by listing the rural charms of Horton's country-side and noting with envy the simple pleasures of its rustics, one hardly feels he succeeded...His house has gone, but we can look about us to see something of the landscape that inspired him, though huge reservoirs now render it even more Piscean. But the old church with Norman pillars and memorials both to him and his mother make it a pensively poetic hour for Zodiac pilgrims.

And if I am allowed to include Milton on this sign, why not Shelley? His early life underscored the area of the Fishes, without actually touching the effigies. He went aged ten to Syon House School, on Capricorn's head but very near Pisces, - and later to Eton, hating both. Though he was a sun-Leo, his extreme shyness, idealism and sensitivity argues for Pisces and/or Neptune prominent in his chart. Leo was roused when provoked by bullying at school, resulting in ungovernable rages. Later on, Leo-like, he became the centre of an admiring circle which he never ceased to try to convert to his wild ideals. His first publication was "St Irvine, or the Rosicrucian" whose mystical philosophy (surely Piscean) was subversive at the time, and filled his publisher with misgivings. It was sent to his father, who held the purse-strings and remonstrated angrily with him, and Shelley, sickened by this rejection, felt a Piscean outcast. He was expelled from Oxford for writing "The Necessity of Atheism." He married Harriet, daughter of a wealthy publican - Pisces again, surely?

But it could be fatal to succumb to Shelley's charm; his first wife drowned herself in the Serpentine when he left her, and another unrequited admirer also committed suicide by a drug overdose. Two Neptunian deaths! His own was equally so. His Piscean passion for sailing was eventually his undoing, for after capsizing several times and surviving, he was eventually drowned off Italy - and his body when washed up was so eaten by fish that he was only identified by the sodden poems in his coat pocket. He was only thirty when he died in 1822, after a turbulent life that makes absorbing reading. Never did an idealist have such a devastating effect on the lives around him.. Try Andre Maurois' biography, "*Ariel*" if you want your withers wrung.

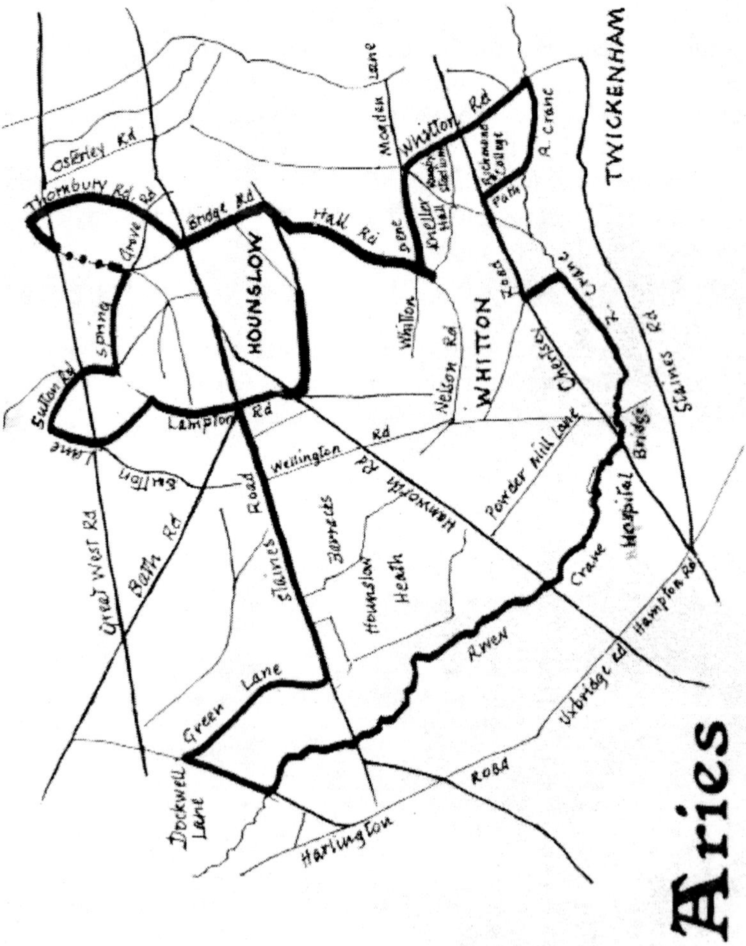
TWICKENHAM
HOUNSLOW
WHITTON
Hounslow Heath
Great West Rd
Bath Rd
Staines Road
Hanworth Rd
Wellington Rd
Powder Mill Lane
Staines Rd
Hampton Rd
Uxbridge Rd
Harlington
Dockwell Lane
Green Lane
Lampton Rd
Sutton Lane
Spring Grove
Osterley Rd
Bridge Rd
Hall Rd
Whitton Rd
Nelson Rd
Morden Lane
Barracks
Hospital Bridge
R. Crane

Aries

Aries

The Ram, generally accounted the first sign of the Zodiac, favours soldiers, being ruled by energetic Mars, god of war. And his influence has not left Whitton and Hounslow unscarred. Celtic war-chariots rode on his back, the Staines road, before the Romans straightened it. This ancient track also outlines Capricorn's back - two ramrods, in both cases signifying discipline, iron determination. From Aries' head Roman roads fan out; so there must have been a Roman camp here. King's Arbour and Caesar's Camp now lie beneath London Airport's runways; a Temple to Mithras, the soldiers' god, was excavated here.

Throughout history armies have assembled on Hounslow Heath; Hounslow Barracks is still here, attesting to a long tradition. As the Syon map says "In this Heathe hath many campes bin pitched, as well by King John as others formerly; as Appeareth by oure Parishe Histories; Wereof the forme of Two yet in parte Remayneth, not far beyond this River, by the Name of Shakesbury Hilles." (Also beneath the airport is a square temple, pre-Roman, and dated to 300 BC., so it should be Druidic.) Were these "hilles" flattened under the airport runways, or if not, where are they? Perhaps one was in Hounslow, where the Bath road forks right from the Staines road, and the Hanworth road, equally Roman, forks left. For the "low" in Hounslow means a mound, after the perverse habit of such old words; and Hounslow is said by some to derive from Hundredslaw, which sounds like a mount of law-giving, the centre of an ancient Hundred or shire. Significantly, the words "low" and "law" seem identical in origin.

Sir Montague Sharpe, whose archaeological researches have done so much for the district, places Hounslow's mound at Smallbury Green.

The martial Knights Templar owned land on Aries, aptly enough; Baber Bridge being one boundary, Hospital Bridge perhaps another. One of their insignia was the Paschal Lamb with head reverted like our sign. You won't find a hospital now at Hospital Bridge over the river Crane on Aries' feet, but the name remembers the Knights Hospitallers of St John, who took over Templar lands when that Order was suppressed. (At Baber Bridge on the Syon map one can't help noticing the intriguing presence of Mother Slipshooes. Did they betray her, making her slip into the Crane? Whoever she was, she has slip-slopped to heaven, some four centuries ago.)

"No Popery" riots gave Catholic James II the excuse to assemble an army of 1600 men on Hounslow Heath to overawe London, but the soldiers were his undoing. He had arrested and sent for trial seven Church of England bishops who had refused to read his "Declaration of Indulgence" from their pulpits, or accede to stuffing Parliament and the higher offices of state with papists. The bishops were acquitted while James was reviewing this army, and he was returning to London, but still within earshot, when he heard great cheers rising from the ranks he had just left. When he was told that they had heard of the bishops' acquittal he realised he had lost his army's allegiance. Knowing that William of Orange was waiting in the wings he had assembled a fleet to oppose him, but a "Protestant Wind" (as it was called) favoured William's fleet and kept James's in port, so he fled abroad with his queen and infant son. This son, so important to James as a Catholic heir, was hailed by papists as a miracle - which seems to indicate that his arrival was unforeseen. And the birth occurred in secret, for James had neglected to confirm it publicly with the usual ritual of attendants and scribes. Consequently Protestants claimed the babe was not his at all, but smuggled into the queen's bedchamber secretly in a warming-pan! So this son did the unfortunate James no good at all, and William of Orange succeeded by virtue of his Stuart wife Mary. But it was the rebellious army on the Heath that made James realise that his cause was lost. Armies are Arian in any case, but a mutinous one especially so - for Aries is famously a rebel.

Highwaymen, also rebels, infested this heath in their day. Where else are they so well remembered?

The flash of flint on gunpowder, the footpad's challenge "Stand and deliver!" - drumming hooves and flying carriage-wheels, fierce courage, insane terror - these are the very essence of Mars, which releases adrenalin, the fluid of fight and flight. Elegant Claude Duval, playing on his pipes and dancing with his fair victims while their scowling escorts paid the piper; Tom King and Dick Turpin, "the sweetest saint in the Newgate Calendar", are all Arian types. For Aries, no sneak-thief, has a gallant air. We have already encountered highwaymen under Aquarius, but it will be remembered that Uranus who rules Aquarius is regarded by astrologers as an octave of Mars. However, the bishop of Raphoe and the following tale show that these predators sometimes suffered surprising reverses. A tailor when challenged meekly gave up his purse, but put his hat on the ground and asked the highwayman to shoot two bullets into it, so that he could pretend afterwards to have put up some resistance, and save his reputation. The highwayman gallantly obliged, but when his adversary's gun was emptied, the tailor pulled out a hidden pistol and demanded not only his money back but the highwayman's weapon too. A true descendant of the cunning little tailor of folklore!

Turpin is a magnet for Zodiac legends; his leap to freedom from the upper window of Colnbrook's Ostrich Inn is surely Aquarian. At Hatton's old Green Man Inn under the lee of

Heath Row they display his hideaway up a chimney. At Hounslow's Nag's Head he escaped the Bow street runners by jumping into a grandfather clock with a secret door at the back, while they peppered its front with shot. But the end for most of these desperadoes was the same; they were hanged and their bodies hung in chains along the roads they had infested. As late as 1800 there were no less than thirteen gallows between Heston and Hounslow alone, festooned with their gruesome remains. But the Staines road had long before been a robbers' lair; as early as 1485 the undergrowth that hid them had to be cleared to a depth of two hundred feet on either side, to give travellers a chance to see them coming and escape.

Aries' foreleg at Whitton stamps out martial rhythms at Sir Godfrey Kneller's splendid Jacobean Kneller Hall, now the Military School of Music. The river Crane draws his underside in a magnificent sweep; his hooves once struck dangerous sparks, for there were gunpowder mills here. Not infrequently they blew up, devastating a wide area with explosions that could be heard in London and registered as seismic shocks even as far as the west country - while arms and legs of those who couldn't hide behind the baffle-mounds in time came raining down from the sky. Gunpowder dilates Aries' nostrils; The Kneller Hall bugles are music in his ear.

But all is peace and beauty now where the old shot-tower reflects in the Crane, and the baffle-mounds, spectacularly intertwined with snaking tree-roots, remember these horrors in tranquillity. Was one of these mounds Whitton's original "ton"? Did mound and river together suggest the site for these mills? Today you can wander along Crane Park beside its river, and take your pick (literally) if you want to find out. But beware of Arian explosions. Whit-ton however is rich in Whit-mounds. Another, half cut away in vertical section, still bulges beneath suburban gardens. This and a sports-ground overshadowed by cedars are all that remains of the Duke of

Argyll's Whitton Park. Was this mound here before he came, or did he raise it himself as an 18th century ducal Folly? The Dukes of Argyll were distinguished soldiers, so they were well placed here.

The war-god Tyw, the Norse equivalent to Mars, is said to lurk in Twickenham's name - and Twickenham is certainly a famous battleground for Rugby, surely the most martial game of all; though its heroes battle now more in mud than blood. Another martial note was provided by German swordsmiths who in the early 1600s came to work at Baber Bridge, where the Staines road crosses the Crane, magnetised no doubt by Aries' influence. Another gunpowder mill flourished there, as if one was not enough. The odd name Baber may have been "beaver", but if so, the beavers, like the Germans, have long gone.

A little further north the lamb's tail is docked at Dockwell Green. His reverted head is outlined by Lampton Lane, leading to the village that used to be spelt *Lamb*ton, suitably enough, on the crown of his head. For though roads have given him two ears, horns are difficult to find. Here too is Spring Grove, now West Thames College, but once the splendid home of Sir Joseph Banks, who among many other experiments introduced merino *sheep* to England, and reared them on Hounslow Heath - an experiment that greatly improved the quality of English wool. The heath had long been used for grazing sheep, as old place-names like Herdintone (Harlington) and Shepiston (Sipson) indicate.

Aries is the pioneer of the Zodiac, and Banks was certainly that. President of the Royal Society from 1778 until his death in 1820, he was a great explorer and a passionate botanist. Inheriting wealth, he fitted out Captain Bligh's ship the"Bounty" for scientific exploration. (Was it rebellious Aries that caused the notorious mutiny?) He had better luck with Captain Cook's ship "Endeavour" and sailed hazardously with him round the world, discovering Australia on the way. Striking a rock on the Great Barrier Reef (Mars square Neptune?) they would have sunk, and the ship was only saved by wrapping a sail padded with oakum and *wool* under its hull. One could say that it was sheep's wool that saved them. He was the first European to see a kangaroo at Botany Bay; which he named for its astonishingly rich flora and fauna; he enriched our knowledge of plant species enormously by bringing specimens back to his own nursery at Spring Grove, and adding to the world-famous collection at Kew. He cultivated the first Banksia rose at his nursery - and is remembered locally by Banksian Way. It was he who suggested Botany Bay as a fine place for the transporting of convicts. Australia's massive sheep-farms are due to him - indeed the colonisation of Australia itself, for it was his enterprise and his money that equipped the voyage of discovery - which was originally fitted out for the purpose of watching the transit of Venus at Tahiti in *April* 1769. Australians, though perhaps not aborigines, should visit his home at Spring Grove as a shrine. He and his sister, who kept house for him, were always dressed in rough wool garments they had made themselves from his sheep, and his eccentric appearance on the Heath once caused Bow Street Runners to arrest him as a footpad. But when they searched his pockets for pistols all they found were frogs, toads, and an assortment of wild plants.

Banks was also involved in another peculiarly Arian enterprise, the first triangulation line for the Ordnance Survey, undertaken in *April*, 1784 by General Roy, with glass tubes laid out over five miles of Hounslow Heath. The word Ordnance and the General in charge shows it as originally a martial enterprise, and its two ends are still marked by upright gun-barrels stuffed with a cannon ball, one at the north entrance of Heathrow Airport, the other at General Roy Close, Hampton Hill. A very important "first" this, for Zodiac enthusiasts, for how could we find earth-Zodiacs without maps? They *should* begin on Aries, the Zodiac's first sign!

There are other "firsts" here. The first Friars in England are said to have settled in Hounslow, on the site of the present parish church. The Syon map notes that it was burnt down; Aries is a fire sign. It is interesting to note that the peaceful friars' main purpose was to gather funds for ransoming prisoners of *war* held hostage.

Another burning is also recorded nearby, though actually on the horn of Capricorn at Isleworth - the palace of Richard, "king of the Romans", the unpopular brother of John of Gaunt - burnt down by a furious London mob.

The first army tank was tried out here, and the first polo game in England was played on the heath between regiments fresh from India. The first aerial customs sheds in the country were erected here to serve the first plane flight to Paris in 1919 from Hounslow Heath. These early flights were dangerous in the extreme, and as the intrepid pilots depended on sight alone to find their way, they sometimes got lost and had to make unscheduled landings in unsuitable places, so crashes were frequent. The first flight to Australia (in a Vickers-Vimy) also took off from the heath, a hazardous journey that took the plane nearly 28 days to arrive.

Mrs. Maltwood assigned Aries in her Glastonbury Zodiac to Gawain, the *first* knight to undertake the Quest of the Grail. Arthur's impetuous nephew, he had Arian traits, being reckless youth personified. Leaping before looking; blown by March winds, drenched by April showers, he makes every mistake in the book, and leaves a trail of desolation behind him. It is typical of Aries that he fails to finish his quest. It was his failure to ask the vital question at Grail Castle that caused the Waste Land, when the king sickened, crops failed, women went bald, streams dried up. And is it not significant that this thoughtless youth, leaving a Waste Land in his wake, should be confronted by the Green Knight, whose name would seem to echo Cernunnos, guardian of the earth? From this encounter he only escaped by the skin of his teeth. Only later when experience has battered Gawain into asking who he is, where he is going and why, does he visit the Grail Castle again. This time his question is ready, and in the earliest legends at least, he redeems himself and the land he has devastated. But Hounslow Heath is still a Waste Land, though largely one of bricks and mortar now - a desert far from deserted. Builders, imitating Gawain's headlong "progress", have failed to ask the vital questions, and so created a vast nowhere-in-particular..Yet there were villages here that could have shown them how to build.

I have been allowed to contribute in a small way to youthful Aries by painting a mural depicting Fairy Tales on the canteen wall of Heathfield Infant School in Powder Mill Lane. Miss Groves, headmistress in the 70s, had already importuned the Twickenham College Art Department to paint the gymnasium wall with characters from nursery rhymes, so the school is unusual in possessing two large murals. Her Arian enterprise deserves to be recorded.

The French scientist Gauquelin, though sceptical of astrology, found to his astonishment that prominent athletes and sportsmen all had Mars featuring prominently in their birth-charts. So is it not a curious coincidence that the only two nationally famous sports centres on this Zodiac, Twickenham's Rugby ground and Wimbledon's Lawn Tennis Courts, are sited on Aries and Scorpio - the two signs ruled by Mars?

The great Ram of Twickenham Still hides along the Crane
Where powder-mills made ball and shot For guns of Crecy's fame.
And when he stamped his mighty foot Explosions shook his frame
While arms and legs came hurtling down Out of the sky like rain.
In London when they heard the sound They thought an earthquake shook the ground.
The old shot-Tower still points aloft With death-defying aim.

He turns his head to watch the sun Set blood-red down to Staines -
Where Britons lost and Romans won The ford across the Thames.
Here Charles and Cromwell, Monmouth, James, Have battled for their right
The plain of Mars at Hounslow Heath Was Aries' fierce delight.
His bushy flanks hid highwaymen Who robbed in broad daylight -
For fright and terror, fight and flight Belong to his domains,
And gallows trees with deadly fruit Hanging from their chains.

Now though the Ram's fierce youth is o'er, He'll rouse himself to hear
The Rugby crowds at Twickenham roar, And join the grandstand cheer,
Though battling now in mud, not blood, They make a game of war.
And the bugle call from Kneller Hall Is music in his ear.

Taurus

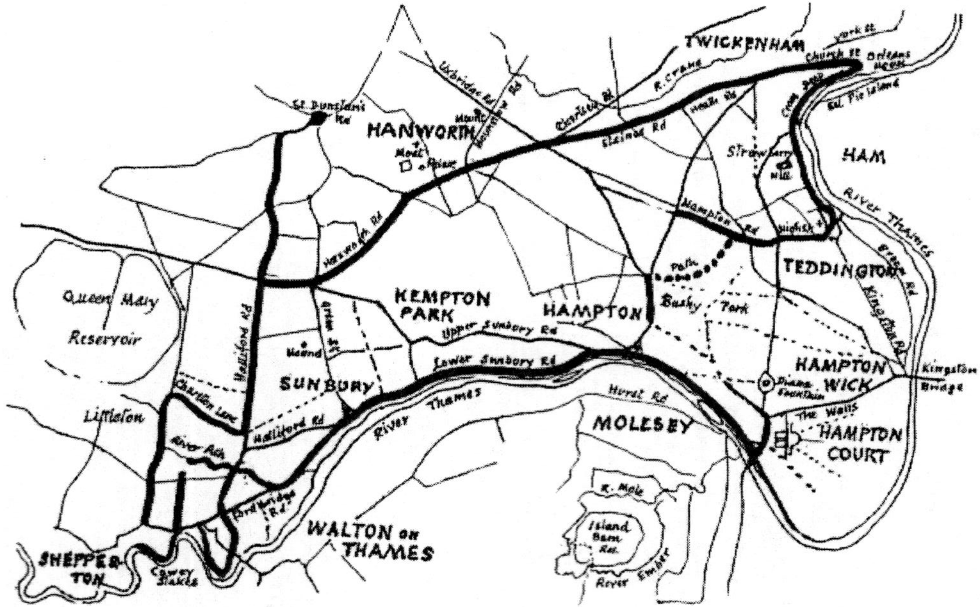
TWICKENHAM
HAM
River Thames
HANWORTH
TEDDINGTON
KEMPTON
PARK
HAMPTON
Bushy Park
Queen Mary
Reservoir
SUNBURY
HAMPTON
WICK
Kingston
Bridge
HAMPTON
COURT
MOLESEY
Littleton
River Thames
WALTON ON
THAMES
SHEPPER
TON
Upper Sunbury Rd
Lower Sunbury Rd
Halliford Rd
Island
Barn
Res.

Taurus

In the Glastonbury Zodiac only the head and foot of the Bull appear, while the Cancerian Ship is much larger. In the Kingston circle the reverse happens; here a leaping bull of enormous vitality and size dwarfs the boat beneath it. The Thames draws his underside from a back foot at Cowey Sale (Yes. *Cowey*) - to Hampton Court, and meets this effigy again to draw his head from Teddington to his horns at Twickenham. Another significant name on this sign that no longer appears on maps were the "Bull Lands" - fields round Twickenham given by Thomas Cole in 1675 for "maintaining a bull for the use of the inhabitants".

Venus who rules Taurus has seen to it that throughout this effigy. The Thames has kept its natural charm, and has even enhanced its bank with noble dwellings, green sloping lawns and beautiful bridges. In fact for astrologers it is notable that both banks of these Thames reaches here are under the influence of the Greater Benefic, Jupiter (Kew, Richmond and Ham), and the Lesser Benefic, Venus, in her two signs of Taurus and Libra. Even Surbiton has been called Queen of Suburbs. And though it has been said that Twickenham's name is derived from Tyw, god of war, this martial aspect only applies to the area north of the Crane which bounds Aries' feet. For Twickenham's old town is on Taurus' head, and it is astonishing how immediately the atmosphere changes from Mars to Venus, under the graceful influence of the Thames. Charming villages, old church towers and elegant mansions one after another, are strung like antique beads on this sparkling silver cord; from Twickenham, through Hampton Court, Hampton, Sunbury, Halliford, where George Eliot and Meredith mused and Thomas Love Peacock swam with Shelley - to Shepperton, a stage-set if ever there was one. No wonder Arts societies and sketching clubs flourish along this stretch of the Thames Valley.

For Venus is goddess of the arts, and for some centuries now has attracted painters, men of letters, playwrights, actors and actresses to live here. She has even seduced poets to Thames' banks from Pisces, whose visual charms cannot compare with hers. Turner lived at Twickenham's Sandicombe Lodge, and delighted in painting the ever-changing sunlight effects on the river. But first in chronological order comes Geoffrey Chaucer who lived for some time at Richmond. Next comes John Donne, the mystical Elizabethan poet who in his youth became one of the Countess of Bradford's coruscating literary circle in Twickenham. This local connection was admittedly of short duration, for he lived in many other places round London. James I, impressed by his sermons, made him Dean of St Paul's. Another mystical poet of Stuart times, Thomas Traherne, lived and wrote in the house of his patron Sir Orlando Bridgeman, in Teddington.

Next we might include Sir John Suckling, poet and dramatist, who was born at Whitton's Kneller Hall in 1609. But we have strayed into Aries - and the Arian influence on this, "the greatest gallant of his time and distinguished by his sparkling wit", is all too plain. Beaten up by a rival in love, he returned the compliment by setting some roughs on the successful suitor. Sir John, a handsome cavalry captain in Charles 1st's army, was engaged in several battles, but being fatally loyal to the doomed king, he was implicated in a plot to save him from execution and had to flee abroad; where having run through his considerable inheritance, he died by suicide, fearing poverty.

Most notable among Twickenham residents was Alexander Pope, doyen of Georgian poets, whose famous Grotto (now much denuded of its shells and stalagmites) is still at Cross Deep, though his riverside garden and Villa has gone.

Though only four and a half feet tall and hunch-backed, Pope's reputation for his translation of the Odyssey and the Iliad - and his waspish wit - was high, and he was visited by all the great of his day, including the Prince of Wales of the time. Pope took John Gay under his patronage, and "taught him the art of rhyming". It is said that Gay wrote his "*Beggar's Opera*" at Pope's Twickenham villa.

Horace Walpole at Strawberry Hill was another who continued the Venusian tradition a little later, making his home a scintillating centre for the literati of his time. (Zodiac researchers will note that this villa marks the Bull's red eye, and it is one of those strange Zodiac coincidences that the place was called Strawberry Hill Shot, for Sagittarius' bow, bent by the Thames, aims point-blank at it from the opposite bank). Before Walpole enlarged the house into his marvellous Gothick extravagance, Colley Cibber, poet, actor and dramatist, lived there. Under his ownership Drury Lane Theatre flourished as never before, and Cibber, though Pope and Samuel Johnson were so rude about his talent, was nevertheless made Poet Laureate. Walpole founded a press there, and published Gray's "*Elegy in a country churchyard*" among other poems.

David Garrick lived in great style at Hampton, embellishing the Thames bank with his noble villa and domed temple to Shakespeare. Tennyson - another and most distinguished Poet Laureate - lived for some time in Montpelier Row; Walter de la Mare also lodged in this terrace - a gem of Georgian architecture. Peg Woffington the actress and toast of her time, graced Teddington, where her cottage near the church still survives. Doone Close now reminds us that Richard Blackmore lived and died in Teddington, where among other novels he wrote his enduring romance "*Lorna Doone.*" Noel Coward lived in Waldegrave Road nearby. Many other lesser-known practitioners of the various arts have graced this effigy, but here are enough to make my point; for where else shall we find so many devoted to the Venusian crafts? The film and television studios at Teddington Lock, Twickenham and Shepperton have continued this tradition, and acted as magnets attracting those in this medium to settle here on this sign.

Taurus is the Builder of the Zodiac. So it is significant that when old Teddington church was found too small for its congregation they built St. Alban's opposite it - not just a church but a veritable cathedral. Half-built just when church-going enthusiasm began to wane, funds ran out, and it was never finished. But it is a noble monument, even so, and being too magnificent to demolish, Venus has since found a use for it as a splendid concert hall.

It is surely curious that the only other ecclesiastical building on such a scale in this Zodiac was Merton Priory on Scorpio, in its time as large as Southwark Cathedral. We have already seen examples of the astrological tendency for signs to reflect across to their opposites. Another instance, though on a microcosmic scale, is the existence of an 18th century pyramid tomb in both Hampton and Wimbledon churchyards. Though I cannot claim to have looked for such monuments in every churchyard in this Zodiac, these are the only ones I have found in this circle. And as the pyramid is the prime symbol of the grandest Builders of all time, I could not help being struck by the fact that they reflected the Taurus-Scorpio axis across this Star-Temple. Taurus the builder v. Scorpio the Destroyer.

Taurus the Builder has of course excelled himself at Hampton Court, the most famous of all the splendid edifices on its effigy. But as most readers will have wandered in it, wondered at it, and been enthralled by its history, I need not expand on it here beyond pointing out its Zodiacal animals on the forecourt (including of course the Bull) - and Henry VIII's Zodiac clock. (It stopped when James I's queen, Anne of Denmark, died.) The maze should be mentioned too, for mazes or labyrinths are of the Mysteries. In the old Greek legend Theseus (the god-man, Theo-Zeus) risked death and saved Athenian youths and maidens from being served up annually as food for the Minotaur who lurked in the depths of Crete's labyrinth. Only he could kill this monster, half-man, half-bull, and this he accomplished attached to Ariadne's ribbon, which, tied at the entrance to the maze, allowed him to find his way out again unscathed. So bulls and mazes go together.

What did this legend mean? Cretan youths and maidens had a fairer form of bull-fighting than is current in Spain today; it was even more dangerous, for they were unarmed, and paintings of the period show that they were trained to take the charging bull by its lowered horns, to be tossed somersaulting over its back. Was this not a graphic demonstration to show how the very force of the desire-nature could be sublimated to propel them heavenward? For Venus, goddess of Desire, is the power behind Taurus' earthy Spring sign. And Ariadne's ribbon? Is it not at once the tradition of moral teaching and the thread of memory and experience, which can save us from repeating our errors when we fail?

Threading the maze on a cathedral floor or village green was a penitential and meditational exercise in mediaeval times; there is an old illustration of monks crawling round one on their knees. They showed our forefathers the true path to avoid getting lost in tempting byways that lead to destruction - and reminded them of the expulsion from Eden, the wanderings of Cain, and the Israelites' forty years in the wilderness of Sinai or Sin.

Earlier still, hills like Glastonbury Tor and Merlin's Mount at Marlborough College were terraced into spiral paths. The terraces on Glastonbury Tor have all the complex returns of a Cretan maze; this suggests a comparable age for their construction, and that its curving ramparts were not designed for defence alone, but to serve the Mysteries. Troy, city of

Truth, was said to be built on this pattern - hence mazes were often called Troy-Towns. There are true mysteries contained in the labyrinth, both mathematical and philosophic; it is found in all parts of the world, and is a mandala that can infinitely repay meditation. It can be no accident that it resembles the human brain. Threading the maze on Winchester's St Catherine's Hill with a companion I remember learning two simple lessons; when I was furthest out and losing hope, it was the very next turn that took me to the centre. Another thought-provoking moment occurred when I found myself passing my companion in the next furrow, but going in the opposite direction - though both of us were aiming at the same goal. The continuous crossing over from the right to the left brain and back again has still other lessons to teach.

There may have been a maze at Hampton Court before the present one, for this area is still known as the Wilderness, and maze and Wilderness were interchangeable terms. The Knights Hospitallers were here before Cardinal Wolsey, for excavations there have revealed foundations of their hospice. And as they inherited Templar possessions when that Order was dissolved, it is possible that they were here first. Someone seems to have thought so at least, for a modern cul-de-sac near Garrick's Villa has been named Templar Close. Both Orders in their travels learnt to fuse in their secret religion the Mysteries of East and West, so an earlier maze, if indeed there was one, would have played a part in it.

Benefic Venus, by attracting kings and queens to Hampton Court, has preserved many green acres of beauty for us in its two great parks; and courtiers magnetised to this royal centre have left Hampton distinguished by a number of splendid houses. Penetrate behind them into Bushy Park and you find yourself in a veritable fairyland of willows, rhododendrons and little waterfalls, with the goddess herself present in her alter ego at Diana's Fountain.

Sibell Penn, Elizabeth and Edward V's nurse, deserves mention here, for she still haunts her house near Hampton church, and has appeared not only at the old Mitre Inn on the bridge but in the Palace itself. She and poor terrified Katherine Howard are among some twenty-five ghosts who have often been heard or seen in its history-haunted galleries. Sibell Penn's spinning wheel has sometimes been heard there, and when a more recent partition wall was knocked down, the wheel itself, covered with dust and cobwebs, was found behind it.

But for more details of local apparitions I must refer you to two booklets - "*Strange Kingston*" and "*Mysterious Kingston*" by Barbara and Tracy Russell, who have compiled an astonishing list of these otherworldly visitations. They record that Sir Christopher Wren, who lived for the last five years of his life and died in the Old Court House opposite the Palace he so largely rebuilt, had a way of reappearing in ghostly form for some years afterwards each February 25th - the anniversary of his death. It seems right that this, the first name in architecture, should still be present in spirit on Taurus the Builder. (Though one can't help being thankful that he didn't succeed in replacing the whole of the Tudor Palace with his Renaissance design).

Hampton Court is not the only place on Taurus that has attracted royalty. James II while Duke of York lived on its horns at Twickenham's splendid York House. His daughters Mary and Anne were born there, and both in turn became queens of England. Luckily for us the mansion has survived to become Twickenham's Council Chambers, so now we can all stroll in its delightful riverside gardens and enjoy the remarkable fountain with its life-sized nymphs and satyrs, sculptured with truly seductive Venusian charm.

There was more royalty at neighbouring Orleans House, named after Louis Philippe, the much-exiled King of France, who fled here on two occasions. A touching tale is told that while he was walking nearby, a stranger doffed his hat to him, so the king asked him who he was. "I keep the Crown, Sire" he answered, meaning the inn (still extant) close by. "Congratulations" said the melancholy refugee, "it's more than I was able to do." It certainly was, for some years after being recalled to France he was banished a third time, and died in Esher's Claremont, where Queen Victoria had given him a refuge.

As Venus in earthy Taurus is at her most seductive, it is not surprising that this effigy has harboured more than its share of royal mistresses. An old inn on Hampton High Street that used to be called the "Maidens Arms" was well named; being conveniently near Hampton Court it gave hospitality to a succession of Henry VIII's favourite ladies.

Henrietta Howard, Duchess of Suffolk and mistress of George II, built beautiful Marble Hill, next to Orleans House on the Thames. Mrs. Fitzherbert, the morganatic wife of George IV, later occupied it. She was not his mistress, but was discarded like one when he was induced to marry a more "suitable" match, the Princess Caroline of Brunswick - lured by his father's promise to pay his huge debts if he consented. (Venus has since found another use for these two mansions - Orleans House now holds regular exhibitions of sculpture and pictures, while Marble Hill hosts outdoor concerts).

George and Caroline reluctantly had one child, but this marriage was a disaster, and in two years the couple parted. He tried to bribe her to go back to Brunswick, but she refused and went to live at Blackheath, where she interested herself in a local orphanage. To give himself grounds for divorce George then accused her of adultery and secretly being the mother of one of its children! She was actually tried for this, but the case collapsed for lack of any evidence - much to the joy of the populace. Poor Caroline wrote him a letter complaining of his treatment of her, and when he didn't deign to reply she published it in *The Times*. He even refused to let her in when she tried to enter Westminster Abbey on his coronation in 1821, and her mortification seems to have been literally fatal, for she died shortly afterwards that same year.

Bushy Park Lodge (now part of the National Physical Laboratory) was built by Charles II, ostensibly for his park-keeper who had been his loyal follower in exile - but secretly as a secluded trysting-place for his many affairs. Later the Duke of Clarence, George IV's brother who afterwards became William IV, lived there happily if impecuniously for many years with his mistress the actress Mrs. Jordan. They had many illegitimate children, and as he was a poor manager financially she had to return to the stage periodically to keep them all. But he in his turn was eventually commanded to marry the princess Adelaide of Saxe-Meiningen, to try and ensure a legitimate successor, and poor Mrs. Jordan was banished to Paris before the royal marriage, where she died alone in poverty.

Hanworth's ancient manor, just off the Bull's back, became a hunting-lodge for Henry VIII. After his death the adolescent Elizabeth was there in the charge of his widow Katherine Parr, who had allowed herself to be swept into the arms of Sir Thomas Seymour, younger brother of the Protector Somerset, indecently soon after Henry died. Ambitious and unscrupulous Thomas had first tried to marry Elizabeth, and when this was forbidden he settled for Katherine Parr instead. But this didn't stop him from bursting into the young Elizabeth's room and subjecting her to distinctly Taurean liberties, romping with her in bed, tickling her and cutting her gown to ribbons. It is said that Katherine aided and abetted him, holding the girl's hands to prevent her resisting; not at all the behaviour we expect from Katherine's otherwise unblemished reputation! But it interesting that this tale should be reported on Taurus' effigy - an illustration of what can happen when the lusty Bull goes rampant. For this and other nefarious doings Thomas lost his head - and serve him right. He had also plotted against his Protector brother, jealous of his power. The old Palace has gone, being replaced with a later building, but the Tudor gardens are still there, making it easy to imagine the unhappy Elizabeth wandering through them, plotting her escape.

Later still the Cornish Killigrew brothers, raffish Restoration dramatists, grew up at Hanworth. Witty, profligate Thomas Killigrew built Drury Lane's first theatre, and was groom to Charles II's busy bedchamber - while his sister became one of that king's many mistresses. Taurus at its most earthy!

Hanworth Mount was used as an ice-box for the palace; but as it stands on the crossing of two old roads, one can't help wondering whether it was not originally a prehistoric ley-mound, for which much later this domestic use was found. About half a mile away from the house, it must have been an inconvenient larder. The moat round the original hunting lodge is reputedly Saxon, but "Han" may be "hen" - Welsh or ancient British meaning "old". So both house and mount may be earlier than Saxon in origin. Climbing up the mount to peer down a hole at the top years ago, I could see the Tudor ice-box bricks within. Since then it has been fenced in, so the passer-by can only view the tip of it now, overgrown with trees.

Nell Gwyn, surely the best-known of all royal mistresses, had a farm at Feltham, bought for her they say by Charles II, and conveniently near Hanworth. She was popular, unlike some of his ladies, and many tales of her wit and presence of mind are told. When her closed carriage left from one assignation it was besieged by a hostile mob, so she popped her head out of the window and shouted "Citizens - I am the king's *Protestant* whore!" At which declaration she was allowed to proceed unmolested. On another occasion, humiliated that Charles had failed to bestow a title on their illegitimate son, she called to the boy in the king's presence "Come here you little bastard!" Charles took the hint, and thereupon made him Duke of St. Albans.

St Dunstan's church at Feltham, rebuilt now, but on the site of a Saxon one erected by that saint himself, is on Taurus' tail-tuft. A perceptive correspondent has pointed out that in astrology the last degrees of Taurus (his tail) indicate vision - or if afflicted, the lack of it. *Dunstan has become patron saint of the blind.* This placing is another of those curiously apt Zodiac coincidences, and makes one wonder how many more are still waiting to be found. This Saxon church is one of several that Dunstan had built round the perimeter of this Zodiac.

I am tempted to include Bedfont in this chapter for the sake of its legend, though it lies north of his effigy. Though seduced by London's insistent advances, its expansive green with a Tudor manor nestling against the old church still retains its old charm. They say here that two beautiful but vain sisters were turned into yew trees cut in the shape of peacocks, those proud Venusian birds, for trampling cruelly on their unhappy suitors' hearts. And there they are, lest you should doubt the tale, a warning to cold-hearted ladies, and still waiting at the churchyard gate for bridegrooms who will never come. Bedfont, on the old Roman (or pre-Roman) road, is certainly ancient; its name is Celtic, meaning "Grave by the spring", and many hoary artefacts have been dug up here. Are these ladies a memory of the unattainable Roman goddess of love?

The road from Twickenham to Staines marks the Bull's back to Sunbury Cross. Nearby is an ancient barrow in a private garden down Rooksmead Road. It is said to be an old boundary mark. Was the sun ceremoniously buried here, at the Kingston Zodiac's western boundary? Many Bronze Age funerary urns have been found nearby, so it seems it was once a popular cemetery. Kempton Park, near here, once had an early hunting lodge; the name was once Kenyngton, meaning king's place. The tale goes that Hardicanute, unworthy son of King Canute, died of a stroke there brought on by over-indulgence in food and drink. Whether this is true or not, it highlights another Taurean weakness, and serves as a warning to natives of this sign.

However, Taurus has a higher side than has appeared so far in this chapter, and it is time to give him his due. Astrologically, more developed Taureans are typically men of substance, constant characters whose feet are planted firmly on the earth, and can be entrusted with great responsibilities. Among Arthur's Round Table knights Taurus must be Sir Ector, who in Malory's "*Morte d'Arthur*" is described as "having great business about London", and to whom Merlin entrusted the new-born babe Arthur. And significantly, Taurus in both Star-Temples oversees the Gemini Babe. Is he not the original Hector, Protector of Troy, city of Truth? And was London where Sir Ector built his prosperous business, not in earlier times called Troynovant - New Troy? Hector-Protector of the nursery rhyme was dressed all in green, which seems to indicate Taurus' spring sign - and his effigy in the Kingston Zodiac was for centuries largely given over until recently to prosperous nursery gardens that fed all London.

Hector-Protector is not the only nursery rhyme that has affinity with Taurus. Is this effigy the cow in "Hey diddle diddle, the cat and the fiddle", that jumped over the moon? For Taurus in both star-temples is over the moon-boat of Cancer, and the litle dog (Canis Minor) that laughed to saee such sport, lies nearby in both Zodiacs at Littleton - the dish being arguably the crescent moon that ran away with the Big Dipper, the spoon.

Another old rhyme, "Little Boy Blue", is specifically connected with Hampton Court. He, his Sheep in the meadow and his

Cow in the corn, are three adjacent Zodiac signs. Is he asleep under the haystack of Rick Pond in Home Park? *For this jingle is said to be a lampoon on worldly Cardinal Wolsey, the negligent shepherd of his flock.* But may he not originally have been the northern Twin, coloured bluer than ever today by two resovoirs, his head still bowed in sleep in the river Mole? Unlike Wolsey, he is the Good Shepherd - not sleeping, but dying for his people.

The old Hundred of Spelthorne - (evocative name!) still holds Taurus in its spell. Where was that Speech-thorn? Was it where the Spelthorne Inn stands today? Perhaps it was at Sunbury Cross, where old Green Lane among other tracks converge upon it. Did Folk-Moots gather beneath it, and what was spelt out under it - Ogham, Runes, or in Christian times, stories from the Bible? These last should have figured the three biblical Josephs.

For in secret Hebrew tradition Joseph is Taurus. In British legend Joseph of Arimathea's sprouting staff was a thorn. All three built to protect their dependants; Pharoah's Joseph, chastely fleeing the Taurean allure of Potiphar's wife, built granaries in time to save all Egypt from famine, Joseph the carpenter build a home in Nazareth for the Virgin, pregnant with seed not of his sowing, and earlier found shelter for her babe in the manger at Bethlehem, the "House of Bread." Joseph, self-gelded, becomes the patient ox who provides the bread for the fatherless and the forlorn.

Joseph of Arimathea's legend tells how he rescued the Virgin's mother Anna from the rocks of Cornwall (or Brittany) when she was in like distress, and brought her in his tin-trading ship safely to Palestine. Later he took the boy Jesus under his wing to Britain, and built the first Christian church there. After the Crucifixion he brought the cup of the Grail to Britain. Egyptian Joseph rescued his family from starvation in Canaan, and took his young brother Benjamin under his wing, by the device of hiding a cup (a forerunner of the Grail?) in his sack of corn. The carpenter housed Christ's body at birth in a wooden manger. The tin-trader housed it at death in his tomb.

Egyptian Joseph was a prophetic dreamer - all Josephs are. When he dreamed of corn sheaves all bowing down to his own sheaf, and interpreted this as his brothers making obeisance to him, his jealous kin threw him into a pit. Joseph the carpenter saved his wife and babe from Herod's massacre of the innocents by a dream, and fled with them to Egypt. Joseph of Arimathea testified to the Resurrection and was also thrown into a pit, being sustained by holy visions, until miraculously rescued and told in a dream to go to Britain. This he accomplished by way of Egypt, after many adventures. In fact all three Josephs are recorded as going into Egypt, that great centre of star-lore. Is this a hint at their Zodiacal significance?
For the core of all their characters is in the Zodiac - where Joseph is the ox of Taurus the bread-winner and protector, guarding the Gemini Babe, who lies by maternal Cancer, within whose constellation are the Manger stars and the stars of Assella, the asses...

So I rejoiced to see Joseph the carpenter with his tool-bag in the stained glass of old Teddington Church, on Taurus' head. There must be high crowns for all Josephs in heaven.

Gemini and Cancer

Before examining these effigies, I should enter a health warning. When I first published a short form of this book some years ago I received a letter from a man whose wife had started the first Twin club in England. They had produced twins soon after moving to Walton-on-Thames, and found so many others there in the same situation that founding a club to help each other out seemed the most practical thing to do. Subsequent research showed that the number of multiple births in the area was rather more than double the national average! I still fondly keep this letter.

Spectacular loops of the river Mole draw the Twins' heads at Molesey and Hersham, the charmingly tip-tilted nose of the northern Twin contrasting strongly with his frowning (or screaming?) brother. This character-contrast colours most Twin myths - Cain and Abel, Castor and Pollux, even Kay and Arthur - though Arthur was only envious Kay's foster-brother. However, all these fraternal sets seem to symbolise our dual human nature, bound in one body yet always at war; conscious and subconscious, animal and divine. The northern Twin, compassionate, all-understanding, is trying to save the other, stretching out his hand along the river Mole to pull him into his boat. But the southern Twin turns his head away as if he didn't want to be saved. Does he not represent our usual mortal state - blind to ourselves yet criticising others, and full of mean tricks?

The original shape of the northern Twin who stretches from Molesey to Walton is now much altered, being largely covered with reservoirs. He is himself a dual figure. For look closer at the rivers that delineate his head at Island Barn reservoir.

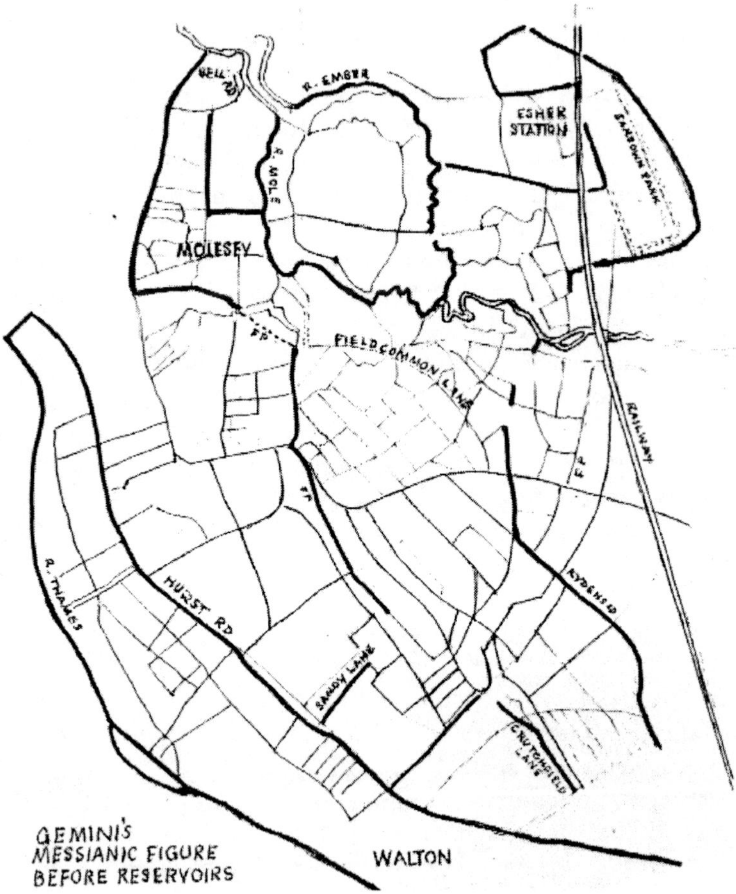
R. EMBER
ESHER STATION
SANDOWN PARK
R. MOLE
MOLESEY
FP
FIELD COMMON LANE
RAILWAY
FP
FP
R. THAMES
HURST RD
RYDENS RD
SANDY LANE
WALTON
GEMINI'S
MESSIANIC FIGURE
BEFORE RESERVOIRS

Mole and Ember together draw a double image - one a boy's head, the other a man's, undeniably Christ-like, and sunk on his chest, his arms now both upraised at Molesey and Sandown Park, as though crucified, or bearing a heavy burden. Both Sandown (Sundown?) and Sunbury just over the Thames seem to see him as the setting sun. Is this Christ bearing the sins of the world on his shoulders, or Atlas, king of Atlantis, bearing the world itself? Perhaps both are the same image, contoured and engraved on the earth, and haunting human consciousness since the dawn of time..

Mind-blowing? Even more so when you realise that the same double image appears in the northern Twin of the Glastonbury Zodiac - though there the messianic head is contoured by Dundon Hill, the profile of the face being drawn by the ramparts of its Bronze Age Camp. Man-made though these ramparts are, they probably follow natural contours, as this would involve the diggers in less work. Either way this double figure must pre-date Christianity by centuries. The head, bent at right angles, seems to be remembered by Lollover Hill (strange name!) that forms the body of this effigy. Is he the Druidic god Esus or Hesus, that Roman Lucan describes as the third person of their Trinity? Old stone sculptures show him as a wood-cutter; Jesus was a carpenter.

The god-name is ancient, and recurs in various forms. The pre-Christian magus Teucros of Babylon, describing the constellation Virgo, says "she has a child in her arms; his name is Ysu." I suspect Isaac who bore his own self-sacrificial faggots up to Mount Moriah, of having the same name, especially as his father Abraham by his name could be seen as Ab-Brahma from Ur of the Chaldees - arguably a father-god prepared to sacrifice his willing son for humanity's sake, before the Jews adopted him as their historical ancestor. The name Ysu, Esus seems to recur in Greek Ul*ysses* or Od*ysseus,* the hero who saved his crew from one disaster after another.

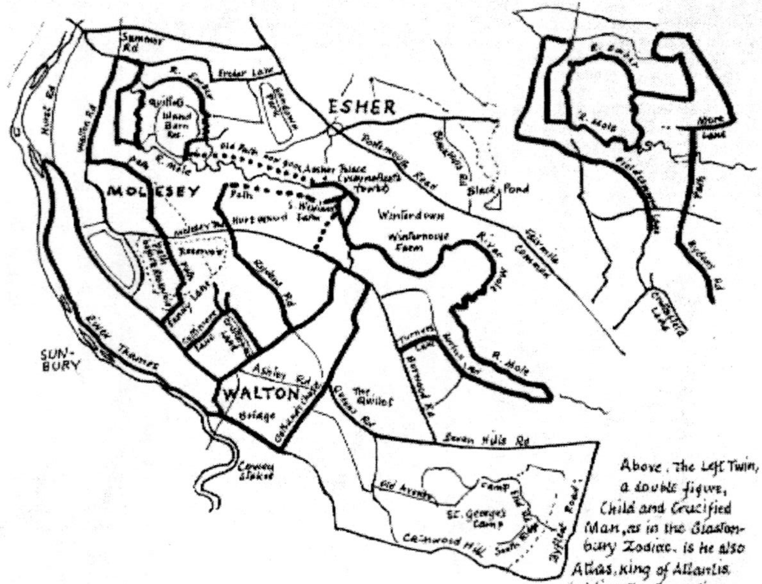

Above. The Left Twin, a double figure, Child and Crucified Man, as in the Glastonbury Zodiac. Is he also Atlas, King of Atlantis, holding the starry firmament upon his shoulders?

Gemini & Cancer

The reservoirs that now cover the northern Twin of Kingston's Zodiac have changed but not totally obliterated his original shape. Alas, Thames Water in the interests of flood prevention at Molesey has recently straightened out the curves of the Mole that for centuries so delicately drew his features, so in the illustrations I have used a pre-1970's map. Esher Council Offices also have large old maps that show this Twin's head and indeed his whole figure before either reservoir was made. I found these a revelation, and was delighted while examining them to find a small pond where his eye should be. But this important feature too has now been obliterated by Island Barn Reservoir. It seems as if this seminal figure is fading fast before the march of progress.

Does Esher remember Celtic Esus? Early forms of this town's name are Aescaron, Essele, Esshere, and place-names books derive them from ash tree, ploughshare, boundary - anything so long as it's boring and meaningless. But they forget that Asser, Alfred the Great's learned Welsh law-maker, biographer and bishop was here, founding Walton church on the crutch of this Twin.(*Is it coincidence merely that Crutchfield Lane leads up to his crutch, or that Hurtwood Road on his side marks the wound of Longinus' lance?*) We know of Alfred's burnt cakes at Athelney from Asser's Life of Afred - a culinary disaster that Mrs. Maltwood explains as no accident, but a ritual of burning barley-cakes fed into the mouth of the great Hound of the Glastonbury circle - a "sop to Cerberus" to enable Alfred to pass safely up the Parret river that draws his underside into the Mysteries of that Zodiac.

Did Asser himself initiate his master into this Secret? Welsh histories claim Asser as Gereint, brother to Morgan Hen, king of South Wales, so as a scion of the royal house he should have known of the Zodiac. Alfred engaged him as tutor to his son Edward (confusingly known as the Elder), and as this Edward was the first king to be crowned on Kingston's Coronation Stone, it is tempting to think that Asser knew of Kingston's

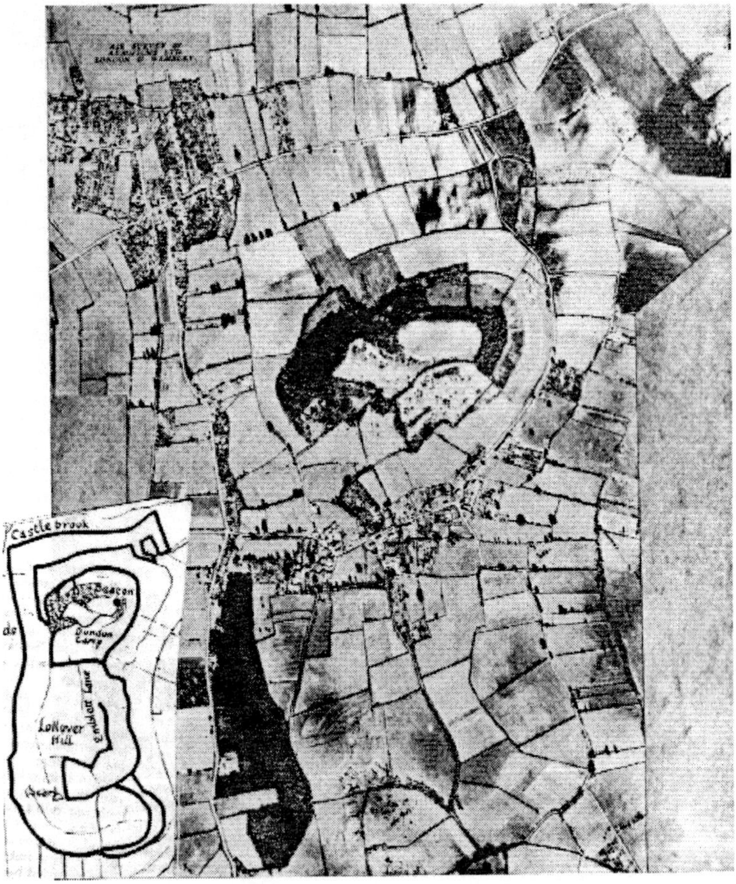

Gemini's dual figure in the Glastonbury Zodiac, the Babe inset and Messianic figure within.

Zodiac also. It is interesting that Alfred chose a Welshman, not a Saxon, to help him define the country's laws and educate his son; it indicates his respect for the indigenous Druidic cultural heritage of the land, so superior to anything his Saxon thanes could provide.

Ashley Park at Walton remembers this royal Welsh bishop; its early name was Asshlees, and the mound on which he built his church was called Bishop's Hill in his memory. So why did he take the name Asser, the sun-god of Assyria, indeed of all Asia? We have already observed how many eastern names recur among the old British kings - a legacy from the Celts' long migration from the region of the Black Sea, and their Phoenician metal-trading connections in Britain. Their Christianity had an eastern Gnostic flavour; Celts could never understand why the Roman Church should rack them for referring to Jesus as Dionysus or Orpheus.

The young and dying Phoenician god Eshmun or Iesu-Munu, would be at home in Esher! One of the reasons the Druids accepted Christianity with comparatively little objection must have been that their god Esus had the same name - and their eastern contacts made them broad churchmen. The way the Welsh pronounce the name Jesus - Yesse - restores lost meaning to the word. The essence of Man. The Latin verb Esse - "to be" -points also to this Man-to-Be. Say Yes and affirm the sacred name - as no doubt our ancestors of long ago did on Dartmoor's highest peak, Yes Tor. So Esher's "Essele" may well remember the universal god-man in the Mole.

The Tree of *Jesse*, often seen in mediaeval stained glass, thus takes on a deeper meaning. Not just the Jewish family tree of Jesse, father of King David and ancestor of Joseph, Mary and Jesus, it becomes a universal symbol of Man's evolutionary struggle through countless ages - its sap or *essence* nourished like a tree, not only from the earth but also from the heavens.

In 1480 Bishop Waynefleet built an episcopal palace on the Mole, just where the Twins' hands join, as a convenient resting-place on his journeys from Winchester to Kingston and London. Its Tudor Tower is still there (privately occupied), though the rest of the once extensive building has disappeared. Cardinal Wolsey was confined in it one winter, after his fall from power, and Shakespeare when he recorded this in his play "*Henry VIII*", called the place Asher House. So as Esher, on whose confines it lies, seems to have been pronounced Asher in Shakespeare's day; I can't help wondering whether Alfred's bishop of the same name was there centuries earlier, thus netting the whole Gemini figure from Asshlees to Esher, and dignifying him with the divine name.

Ahura, god of the Medes and Persians, is shown with the same winged sun-disc as Asshur. Both names contain techniques for enhancing consciousness. An old London Druid told me that A-hura (strangely like Arthur) was a deep-breathing name, in for A, out for Hura. Such exercises persist in Indian yoga, which has never lost these Indo-Aryan traditions. But Asshur, he said, means more. The extra s's are the Kundalini serpents which by such means can be induced to creep up the spine (as in Asclepius' and Mercury's caduceus) to illuminate the pineal cone in the brain and give not only holistic health but inspiration.

And who has not seen sculptured Assyrian priests lustrating the Tree of Life (the spine) with the sacred pine cone? Phoenician Asclepius who was killed by Zeus for the heinous crime of resurrecting a man from the dead, became the Greek god of healing, even of resurrection, and his name surely echoes Asshur. He travelled north, appearing in Norse myth as Ask, the first man, made from an ash tree. Odin, his creator, hung nine days on the great Cosmic ash tree Ygdrasil, whose roots were in Hell, its trunk in Middle Earth, its branches in Asgers heaven. The concept of the crucified god is older than Christianity. Who knows? He may even go back to suffering Atlas of Atlantis. So we may forgive the place-name books for tracing Esher's name back to the ash; there seems to be more to this tree than wood, and its ash-keys can unlock long-lost secrets.

Did William Lilly, the famous astrologer who among many astonishingly accurate prophecies predicted the Great Fire of London, know of this Zodiac? He lived and died in Walton, and his friend Elias *Ashmole* of Oxford's Ashmolean gave him a memorial stone in Walton church's chancel. William used to travel weekly to Kingston Market, where he generously gave out herbal remedies to any who needed them. But he was in trouble when his prediction of London's Fire of 1666 proved all too accurate, for he was summoned before a committee and accused of starting it himself in order to see his prophecy fulfilled. He must have confused them still further when he asserted that he had also foreseen the Plague of London of 1665. But influential friends vouched for his integrity, and the accusations were dropped. When he first predicted the fire in 1651 he accompanied it with a drawing of the Twins falling head-first into flames, because London is astrologically under the sign of Gemini. The Twins seem to have been fateful for him, living as he did on Gemini of the Kingston Zodiac. Did his drawing of a mole creeping up a river to a crown (reproduced here) remember the Man of the Mole aspiring to an immortal crown? Or was it merely a memory of banished Bolingbroke, (as historians say) who once lived at Walton Manor, and returned to unseat Richard II and seize the crown as Henry IV?

The Mole and Ember rivers, once called the Amele and Imele respectively, named the whole Hundred of Amelebrugge in Saxon times; it is now called Elmbridge. The Deanery that contains this Twin's head has the old name of Emly. And in view of the fact that between them these rivers delineate this Twin's remarkable head, they may provide him with yet another eastern name, and a highly significant one. The

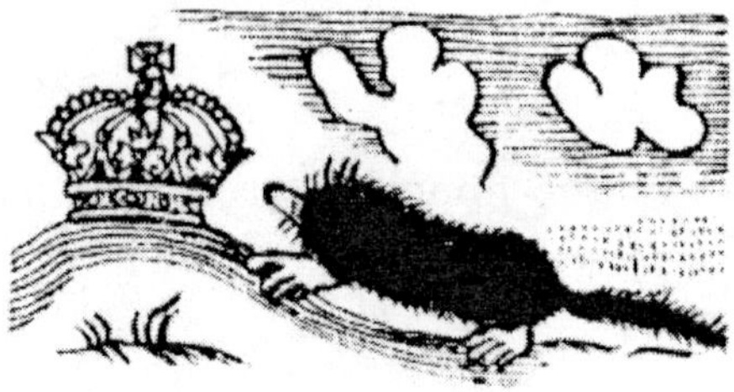

pedigree of Owen, son of Welsh Howell the Good (d. 848 AD) traces back to "Aballac, son of Amalek, son of Beli the Great and his wife Anna, who it is said was the cousin of the Virgin Mary, mother of our Lord Jhesu Christ." Robert Graves, noting this remarkable statement in his "*White Goddess*", says "If it stands for Abimelech son of Amalek son of Baal and Anatha, it commemorates a tradition that the (British) family were formerly lords of Canaanite Shechem" .

Nor is Howell's the only Welsh family tree with this astonishing connection; several have it. One even claims Anna as the *mother* of the Virgin...The Amalekites are censured in the Old Testament as foes of the Israelites invading Palestine, so they were there before them, and not unnaturally resented the immigration. It certainly looks as if some of them joined with the Phoenician metal-traders to Britain, and remained, intermarrying no doubt with the indigenous royal family.

So what can the name Amalek mean? Melek is Phoenician for "king", and the root amo- means love. In the context of the Kingston Zodiac's northern Twin it is tempting to see the name as the King of Love...

One old MS in Jesus College (the Welshmens') states that "the woman Anna was of the Hebrews who dwelt at Holy Oak, and sought their fortune in gold". Was this the princess Anna, pregnant and turned out of doors by her heartless husband, that Joseph of Arimathea the tin-trader rescued from the rocks of Cornwall and took to Palestine? Until recently this tale was still whispered in Cornwall, which has several old chapels dedicated to her, and it is still repeated out loud in Brittany where St. Anna is their chief patron saint, still celebrated in country districts with processional Pardons. They locate her rescue on Breton cliffs of course, and in their version of the legend Joseph is not mentioned - her rescuer becomes an angel. They also say that in old age she returned to be their Duchesse, and was greatly beloved for giving her possessions freely to the poor. They claim too that her grandson Jesus visited her (on one of his uncle Joseph's trading missions?) before she died.

While grateful to the Bretons for preserving much that we have sadly lost, it must be claimed that this tradition probably came originally from Cornwall, when Brittany was flooded with British soldiers under the general Clemens Valerius Maximus in the 380s AD, who fought in Gaul to become Roman Emperor of the West. He only lasted nine months in the purple before he was killed by a rival, and is blamed for denuding Britain of her fighting men and thus rendering her helpless before the Saxon invasions. For his army never returned, and its royal leaders henceforth became kings of Brittany - "Little Britain".

In Malory's "*Morte d'Arthur*" Joseph of Arimathea meets with Avallach or Aballac - who he calls Evelake - on the borders of Canaan and Egypt, just as he is setting out for the West, soon after the Crucifixion. He helps Evelake overcome his enemy Tolleme (obviously a Ptolemy) by giving him a wondrous shield on which at the height of the battle appears a picture of the Saviour crucified. At this vision his enemies flee in fear - and Evelake, hitherto a Saracen of Sarras, gratefully embraces Christianity. Devoted henceforth to Joseph, he insists "whether he will or no" in accompanying him to Britain. Here he enters the old Welsh king-lists as Avallach,

Joseph Rescues Princess Anna of Cornwall by Mary Caine

presumably of Avalon. In fact in Malory's account (which he took from the earlier "Saint Graal") Evelake/Avallach is the Maimed king of the Grail. Maimed by approaching too near its Mysteries, he is doomed to linger through the centuries until Galahad his perfected descendant arrives in the fullness of time to heal him.

Though this account ignores the Welsh king-lists that show Avallach's grandfather Beli and wife Anna as already King and Queen in Britain, at least it emphasises the tradition that the family were Canaanite (Amalekite?) in origin. The name Beli or Belin is that of eastern Baal. It also strengthens the case for Joseph of Arimathea coming to this island. If this family came to Britain with the Phoenicians to make their fortune in metal-trading, why not Joseph too? He was a rich man in the Gospels, and may well have been related to them.

Were they Canaanites or Hebrews? The name Belin argues for the former - Market Jew Street in Penzance and the name Marazion for the latter. The remains of open-cast mines in Penwith were long known as "Jews' leavings". But the tribe of *Asher*, (one of the 12 tribes of Israel) was much mixed with Canaanites (as their name, interesting in the context of this chapter, implies), and according to the Old Testament provided men for the Phoenician king Hiram's trading ships way back in Solomon's time. So perhaps it is unnecessary to draw any distinction.

Amalek's son in the genealogy quoted by Graves is Abimelech; so it is curious that the old names of the two rivers that draw the Kingston Twin's head - the Amele and the Imele - echo this relationship. Ab or ap means "son of". Old Imber Court, pulled down and now a police headquarters in Molesey, still preserves this name. Odd too, that Ember Lane draws the Gemini figure round Lollover Hill in the Glastonbury Zodiac.

Apps Court, an ancient manor in Hurst Road, between this Twin's figure and the Cancerian Boat, is interesting in this context. Spelt Abbs in the 17th century, Ebsa in Domeday Book, it was in Saxon times granted to Chertsey Abbey; but though through the centuries it has had many owners, none of them has a name even faintly resembling any of these variations. The possibility then arises that it could originally have been Ap or Ab - Youth, Son - a reference in the old Welsh tongue to our northern Twin. ("Mab" in the Mabinogion has the same meaning.) This possibility is strengthened by the fact that Apps Court is in the parish of Walton-on-Thames, the Waellas' town. Its church was dedicated to St. Mary in Alfred's time by the princely Welsh bishop Asser. It is as if he knew that Walton was on Cancer, the maternal sign of the Zodiac, and that its Boat contained her Son.

"Little Sir William" the hapless victim of an old folk-song, sheds more light on the sun-god of the Mole, though it comes (intriguingly enough) from Somerset. For William derives from another Celtic sun-god name that will help to explain another couple of enigmatic names on the Twins of the Kingston Zodiac. So this sad song must be given here.

Easter Day was a holiday   Of all days in the year
And all the little schoolfellows went out to play
But Sir William was not there.
Mama went to the Jew's wife's house And knocked at the ring
Saying "Little Sir William, if you are there
Pray let your mother in."
The Jew's wife came to the door and said
"He is not here today
He's with the little schoolfellows out on the green
Playing some pretty play."
Mama went to the Boyne Water
That is so wide and deep
Saying "Little Sir William if you are there
Pray pity your mother's weep."

"How can I pity your weep, Mama And I so long in pain?
For the little penknife sticks close to my heart,
And the Jew's wife hath me slain.
Go home, go home, my mother dear
And prepare my winding sheet,
For tomorrow morning before eight o'clock
You with my body shall meet.
And lay my prayer book at my head
And my grammar at my feet
That all the little schoolfellows as they pass by
May read them for my sake."

This may be a dirge for the Glastonbury Gemini Boy, for I was told long ago by a Zodiac researcher who lived there that in past times there were "Dirge Singers of Dundon." Yet oddly enough it fits Kingston's Boy better, for he is indeed lying in a river. And if the Mole is not the Boyne, there is by strange coincidence in Walton church a huge baroque memorial to Lord Shannon, victor of the Battle of the Boyne. Another of those Zodiacal quirks! The dirge may of course have come from Ireland with the monks who flooded from there to Glastonbury. Or should we read Boyne as "Boy's" water?

Sad songs of murdered young boys proliferated in the Middle Ages; Little St Hugh of Lincoln was another victim, - and a little Sir Hugh was also mourned in Scotland. Chaucer's Prioress told a similar tale. In her version Jews cut the throat of a little boy who persisted in singing a Christian song in their ghetto, and threw him into a pit. The Virgin however put a grain of corn in his mouth, which enabled him to continue singing despite his severed vocal cords, until his weeping mother heard it and found him. Is this not an echo of primaeval John Barleycorn, the sun-and seed god who resurrects after being put in the ground to die? And is the Virgin with her grain of corn not the earth-mother Virgo of the Zodiac with her wheatsheaf?

For this reason, and because two of the victims have Celtic sun-names (William comes from Hwyll or Haul the sun, and *Hu* Gadarn, another divine ancestor, led the Cymry west to Britain following its setting path). I believe these dirges are older than mediaeval, and were popular folk-memories of the pre-Christian dying young sun-god of Druidic Zodiacs.

Pwyll in the Welsh Mabinogion tales became king-for-a-year in the Underworld; he must have been Hwyll ap-Hwyll, son of the *Wheel* of the sun, and reflected on earth, or dying, in a *pool* - and like Greek Helios giving us Will, Weal, Wealth, and Health. (St. Patrick, in times when Ireland still had Druids, records how he threw off an oppressive incubus one night by crying "Helias! Helias!") The Long Man of *Wilm*ington near *Will*ingdon Hill is said to be the sun opening the doors of day. Brown Willy, Bodmin Moor's highest point, and Dartmoor's High Willhays next Yes Tor must remember him.

The dirge quoted above is a fascinating mixture of Celtic and Christian ideas. Little Sir William dies and reappears like Christ to Mary Magdalen and his mother at Easter, the only Christian festival whose date, Celtic style, depends on the moon. But Jesus did not die while still a boy with a penknife in his heart. Yet if we read "quill" for pen, it becomes a pun on Hwyll's own name. Here is another reason for suspecting that these songs were originally in the Celtic tongue and were translated into English in mediaeval Christian times, when the anti-semitic theme was added to explain the lunar goddess's death role. The *pen*knife or quill could then become Cupid's feathered arrow in the God of Love's own heart, shot from Sagittarius' bow; a last sun-ray from the divine father illuminating his son. And when in his turn he sets, the very *will*ows mourn his passing.

The enigmatic name Quillots, an old house near the northern Twin's head, and the Quillets on his brother's seat at Hersham, can now take on new meaning. The name, according to geologists, denotes Celtic fields. Could they recall those sacred fields which like a *quilt* cover the recumbent Twins? While wondering on this, I visited the old Bell Inn at Molesey, lured by its half-timbered eaves that lean drunkenly at all angles. Within to my astonishment I found the walls lined with old local land-auction bills, all described as Lots. They were Will or Quill-lots - Hwyll-lots! (Was this visit another of those well-timed Zodiac coincidences? For when I returned there a year later I found these had gone.) But I can still recommend this charming old tavern to thirsty Zodiac pilgrims. Just round the corner stands the period house called the Quillots, on the way to the *will*owed Mole.

And the Jew's wife - is she the murderess she seems? No. As the moon she simply marked the time of his death. Malory in his section on the Grail explains her role. Solomon, he tells, was advised by his "evil wife" to make a ship durable enough to sail through the centuries, as a way of preserving his ineffable wisdom and bearing it through the seas of time to generations still unborn. Through his contact with Hiram of Tyre that wisdom was quabalistic, astrological. But Solomon by his name means the sun, so his wife must be the fickle moon. In mediaeval days this lunar "Jewess" was used to feed anti-semitism - a prejudice which was profitable both to Church and State, since it encouraged both to strip the Jews of their wealth without feeling too much guilt. But this sadly degraded her original lunar role, which is to mark the timing of events - of birth and death - and Easter. In the fullness of time Galahad the Christ-like knight and his aspiring follower Perceval (surely our Twins) board Solomon's lunar ship and sail away to Sarras to achieve the Grail.

We have seen that Evelake/Avallach is said to have come from Sarras, on the north-eastern border of Egypt. Malory calls Tolleme (obviously an Egyptian Pharaoh) a Saracen too. Sarras means stars, and Saracens are those who worship the stars. The folk-name Sarsen stones which our forbears gave to monoliths and megalithic circles remembers their star-orientation - for the Welsh for star is "Ser". So when Galahad sailed away to Sarras in Solomon' Ship to achieve the Grail a higher star-city must be meant; a greatly raised state of consciousness and understanding - not merely a geographical location, however steeped in star-lore that might be. While on board he could absorb the ancient secrets the ship contained; secrets which themselves had the power to raise his consciousness.

In the context of these Star-Temple Zodiacs it might be said that he and his companion are already there at Star City, and need not move from the spot.

The northern Twin is full of light; Summer Lane and Lammas Lane proclaim it - Lammas or Lugnasad being a Celtic summer festival. But Winterdown, Blackhills and Black Pond surround his benighted brother.

South Weylands Farm on the effigy of this 2nd Twin hints that he may be Weyland the Smith, the land between the rivers Mole and Wey being his by right. Weyland's origins are said to be Teutonic, so perhaps that is the later name that Saxons, apprised of this effigy and his character, gave him. In essence he is one with Vulcan, the son of Zeus cast out of Olympus, lamed and rendered ill-tempered by his fall, doomed to work his passage by metal-working in the bowels of the earth. Or Castor (whose name suggests he was cast out too) the mortal Twin of immortal Pollux. When all too human Castor died, Pollux begged Zeus for his life, and was told that they could live alternately on earth, if Pollux was prepared to sacrifice his own immortality for him. This he was prepared to do, and Zeus, touched by this brotherly love, translated them both to the sky as the Twins. An intriguing case of Christian ideals centuries before Christ?

And is he not also Cain, cast out and branded for enviously murdering his innocent brother Abel? Tubal-Cain of Genesis was, like Vulcan, a metal-worker. No accident, surely, that Caen Wood is on his seat. This name is not lost on me, for it is my own. This mortal twin must work his ill-tempered way back to salvation by burrowing in the earth (self analysis?) until by patient alchemy he can work his gross-metalled nature into gold.

His effigy appears clearly in the air-photo, because it lies on unbuilt land. His head lies beneath a deep cliff burrowed by the Mole; looking down on it from woodland near the Portsmouth road's Fairmile, it is indeed as if he had been cast down to earth. (Was it this morose giant who smashed those windscreens on the Fairmile some years back?)

Cain in the Bible was the first tiller of the soil; Burwood Road in Walton is perhaps his spade haft. By odd coincidence those Puritan simple-lifers the Levellers or Diggers took possession of the old British Camp of St. George's Hill, just beneath this effigy,on ramparts built by earlier diggers still. They must have reasoned that this old Camp belonged to no-one in particular; but scandalised neighbours, alarmed at this early experiment in Communism, soon took them to court and had them thrown off the hill. They too were "cast down." Ironically, the camp is now the haunt of stockbrokerdom, and qualifies for the title of Brass Buckle on Surrey's Cocktail Belt. There's gold in them thar hills!

This fallen Twin needs his brother's helping hand to save him, but turns his obstinate head away like the sinking man who got his grammar wrong, shouting "I *will* drown and nobody shall save me." At least St Peter when he failed in his attempt to walk on the water allowed his Saviour to pull him into the boat.

Cancer

As there is no Crab to be seen in either earth-Zodiac, this boat replaces it - as does the splendid Ship in the Glastonbury Zodiac. And though this craft at Molesey is a mere canoe compared with its Somerset counterpart, at least it floats on the Thames, allowing pilgrims to float with it and enjoy delightful scenery as they reflect on its Mysteries. Cancer is the Zodiac's maternal sign, ruled by the moon, and as this vessel contains a child and is crescent- shaped, it performs its Cancerian function better than the Crab could ever do. It can also be said to represent the constellation of Jason's Argo, near neighbour of Gemini in the night sky.

Jason's legend is undoubtedly Zodiacal, for besides numbering the Twins Castor and Pollux among his crew he sought Aries' Golden Fleece and won it in the teeth of its stellar guardian, circumpolar Draco. But if like Odysseus' voyages his adventures were once a Pilgrim's Progress through the temptations of the Zodiac signs, his legend as it has come down to us has degenerated sadly from its original form, for he succumbed to many of its tests, not least to the deadly charm of Medea, a fiend in female form. Perhaps his savage adventures were an Awful Warning? He seems to have lost his way after spectacular beginnings. Tired of life, he lay down under his beached ship, and its poop fell upon him while he slept, crushing him to death. Was he a failed initiate? Whether he was or not, the picture the 1st Twin gives, sleeping or dead with bent head beneath the Argo's poop, is reminiscent that of Gemini in both earth-Zodiacs.

Isis and the Christian Virgin have both long been pictured in a crescent lunar vessel in the sky, which symbolises at once moon womb and tomb; its pale goddess marking the time and place for Man's birth, his voyage through life to death and rebirth. Solomon's ship in Morte d'Arthur, initiated by his intuitive moon-wife -echoes this.

We have already seen that these stars portray the Bethlehem scene, with Joseph as the Taurean ox, Gemini the Babe and Cancer herself as the Virgin mother. And the most obvious hint of all that Astrology is involved in this scene is the story of the Three Magi, led there by a star. The astronomer Kepler identified this "Star" as a close conjunction of Jupiter and Saturn, which occurred in Pisces no less than three times in 7 BC; Jupiter the Greater Benefic, Lord of Heaven, rules Pisces, and Saturn is the ruling planet of the Jews.

The Assella stars, the ass in this birth tableau, also seem to presage Jesus' approaching death, for at the onset of his Passion we are told that Jesus chose an ass and her foal for his triumphal entry into Jerusalem. Was he consciously re-enacting the ancient star-pattern? For these same constellations also show the Crucifixion scene, with great Orion as the dying Christ, Gemini's two robbers beside him. (Mercury who rules Gemini, is astrologically the god of thieves). One of these is all too mortal, railing at his dying Saviour, while the other is judged immortal. This pattern is emphasised in Glastonbury's Star-Temple, where Orion's stars overlay the northern Twin when the planisphere is superimposed to scale over the map. It is emphasised also as we have seen by the Christ-like head and figure that appears within that of the northern Twin in both Zodiacs.

It is extremely curious that the earliest authorities on the date of the Crucifixion, Hippolytus, Lactantius and Tertullian among them, state that the Crucifixion (and thus the date of Easter) occurred in the last years of the emperor Tiberius - when "the two Gemini" were consuls in Rome (See *Encyclopedia Britannica*, IIth ed., under "Bible".) Why should they have emphasised this dual consulship? Did they see it as astrologically significant?

Jesus also instructed his disciples to follow a man with a waterpot to the upper room where they were to hold the Last

Supper. Was this not Aquarius, symbolising that the grave was not the end? And when he appeared to them after the Crucifixion it was again in an upper room, Aquarius' position in the Zodiac, and the sign of Resurrection. And when he appeared by the lake before his Ascension and prepared a meal of *fish* as a farewell repast for his friends, was this not a sign of dissolving Pisces? A sign too that the Saviour of the Piscean Age was about to leave this earth?

If Jesus and his cousin John the Baptist were Essenes, as many Biblical researchers now think, he may well have chosen to follow the star-pattern of salvation; for the Essenes, like the Pythagoreans they resembled, revered and taught the ancient wisdom of Astrology.

It may amuse you to see this work signed by the name Caine - most benighted of all the effigies. As it really is my name and not a nom-de-plume like Asser's, it demonstrates (to me at least) with peculiar force the nature of this quest, which is to find and face ones' self. It is typical of the coincidences, miracles even, that attend the pilgrim's way - and gives hope that eventually this far-off goal will be attained. On this often painful Jacob's ladder angels too pass up and down, giving a helping hand here, or an admonitory kick from behind, there. And when we tire or fear to fall, we often find that we have been brushed "accidentally" by an invigorating wing.

Conclusion

When I was young - a long time ago now, we took for granted that the night sky was a diamond-studded spectacle; so full of stars that there was hardly any space between them. My great-uncle in Devon was able to teach me all the constellations in the Northern Hemisphere by direct observation. Alas, we who live nowadays in the ever more polluted atmosphere of cities have been robbed of this essential window on wonder, and the atmospheric blanket is also obscuring our cosmological view. It is a parable of what is happening to our souls. Nocturnal travellers approaching London's vast illuminated area by plane see something of the brilliance that was the birthright of preceding generations, though now stretched out over the ground. It is as if the stars had all fallen to earth.

Our ancestors had a great advantage over us, in that this awe-inspiring heavenly display, slowly moving round above their heads, was a palpable experience. It joined them to the cosmos; they felt that they were part of a numinous whole that interacted with their own lives and destinies. Today the fading of the stars coupled with (and caused by) the spread of materialism, has given us a very different perspective. Though we are far more comfortable than they, cushioned as we are by the advances of science, we have lost that sense of the numinous, of being part of a meaningful Whole that sustained them and gave them hope and a sense of divine purpose. Religion, which expressed this mythologically, a language we have lost, is fading with the stars. Today our only hope it seems to us is to succeed in the rat race by whatever means we can, and law and morality suffer as a consequence.

Our sense of loss, of separation, if unfocussed, is deep, and we are learning to compensate - many by the use of consciousness-raising drugs. The practice of Astrology and meditation are better ways of doing this, and their growing popularity is significant.

Is it not curious that just as the stars are fading from our sight, Terrestrial Zodiacs have been discovered? And just as traditional religion is being rejected by so many, the story these Star-Temples tell restates these despised doctrines in a new and coherent way. It is true that the constellations have always had their legends, but those preserved by the ancient Greeks and Romans are various, unconnected and often degrading to the gods. Zeus in these legends appeared as sometimes no better than a libidinous old man, and jealous goddesses could be vengeful - not only to each other but to their human victims. In fact it has been said that it was their deplorable behaviour that eventually discredited them, for mankind could no longer look up to them as ideals.

But the subtle changes in these newly-found Zodiac effigies have restored the original and divine meaning to many of these legends, and for this we must thank Katharine Maltwood. For these signs, reinterpreted, reveal the ancient and universal saga of the sun-king, whose self-giving is a pattern to which all humanity aspires - *and is the source of all myths, all religions.*

In discovering the Sagittarian figure of the Glastonbury Zodiac as a mounted sun-king dragged from his horse below the horizon nightly and annually by the Whale in Pisces, she makes sense of the senseless centaur. Her Dove, flying from the sun-god's head to fecundate Virgo the earth-goddess, replaces and improves on the Libran Scales, illuminating the ancient - and pre-Christian - doctrine of the Virgin Birth. For it explains this as the origin of all life on earth by the agency of sunrays and solar winds on our globe. And not physical life only, for the inspirational nature of the Dove promises also a continuing infusion of increasing consciousness on those higher forms of life able to absorb its message.

By removing the fourth human figure of the Water-Carrier of Aquarius and replacing it with a bowl-shaped eagle or Phoenix, the timeless Trinity of all the earliest religions appears, spread over the circle in an equilateral triangle. For the only human signs left on these terrestrial Zodiacs are God the Sagittarian Creator, his consort at Virgo and their son(s) the Gemini Twins, whose dual sign, at present divided in two as mortal and immortal, is destined in the course of divine Evolution to become one. My own discoveries of Gemini's Messianic head engraved in the earth in the northern figure in *both* Zodiacs - surely a coincidence too extraordinary to be meaningless - further confirm this reading.

This "Family Trinity" is its most ancient form, and not only restores womanhood to a creative place long denied in most traditions; it also reveals this ancient doctrine as central to its teachings. The Trinity is a concept whose pattern has long ceased to be discerned in traditional Zodiacs, but its mysterious teachings are ancient, and profound. The essentially triple nature of the creative process was recognised from east to west by both Chaldeans and Druids in their Triads.

Two examples come of its action come to mind to mere tyros like myself in both light and sound - the three primary colours from which the whole spectrum can be spun, and the "three-cord trick" in music, from which all harmonies can be developed. But those are able to delve into the arcane mysteries of number, among them Bligh Bond, John Michell and Gordon Strachan, (to mention only three), are revealing divine wonders in this field which go to the very heart of Creation.

Christians have long left this Mystery alone, as inexplicable. But today it seems there are a few who are able to open the window on Divine Mathematics once more, giving us a new and revelatory view of its ancient wisdom as it survived, mostly in secret, through the ages. Such studies incidentally do much to reconcile Science with Religion; an urgent task if we are to recover a holistic Cosmology that will restore meaning to our lives.

To reconcile apparently opposed religions to each other is another urgent need in our present multicultural melting-pot, and here too these Terrestrial Zodiacs have a real contribution to make. Indeed, Astrology has been a philosophy common to all developed cultures from the earliest times, all over the world, evolving from contemplation of the night sky, itself a mystical experience common to all humanity.

Terrestrial Star-temples are startling concepts; so startling to our present climate of thought that many dismiss them out of hand without examining the evidence. Their very size creates a shock of impact that creates an answering wave of incredulity. But recent discoveries in many fields imply that our forbears had capacities much greater than we have hitherto suspected, and built to mark the passage of the heavenly bodies. Bronze Age temples in many lands are found to be orientated on various stars, as well as the sun or moon. But even earlier, megalithic stone circles, as Professor Thom's intensive measurements show, reveal astonishing sophistication in their construction, based on Pythagorean triangles - long before Pythagoras. They also demonstrate that they were orientated as calendar-markers not only to the movements of the sun or moon, but often to the greater magnitude stars as well. So the practice of marking the stars on earth has been established from the earliest times.

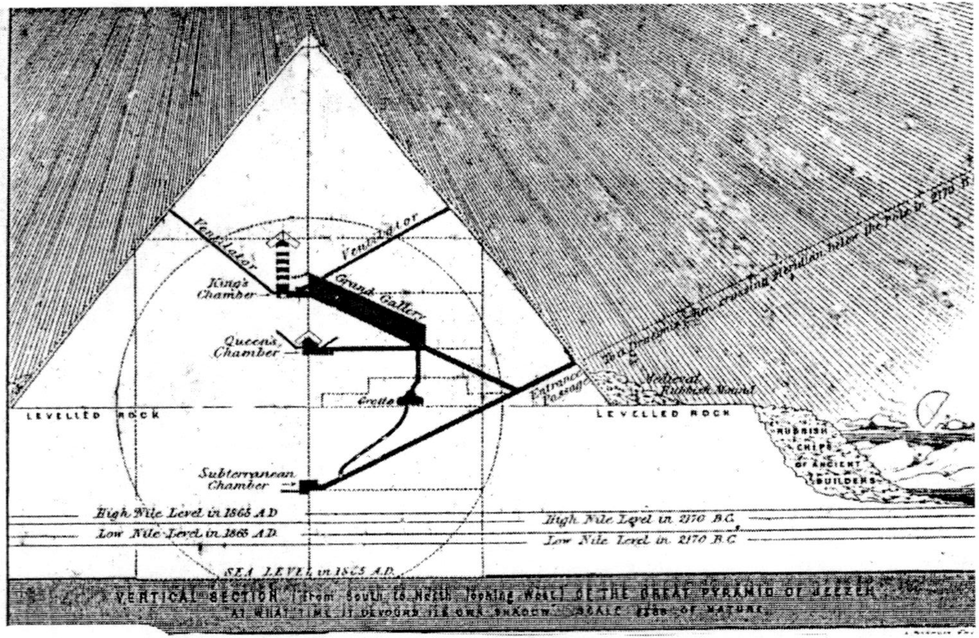

THE GREAT PYRAMID

Both he and John Michell have demonstrated the astonishing hidden mathematical and astronomical wonders of Stonehenge and Avebury, and many have discovered - and are still discovering - Cosmic mysteries in the Great Pyramid. The distance of the earth from the sun, the circumference and diameter of the earth, its relative size to the moon, are but a few of the astonishing measurements that have been detected in that grandly mysterious monument, whose proportions betray the use of that ubiquitous "Pythagorean" triangle, and the geometry of the Golden Mean. This Pyramid's orientation due north and south shows a knowledge and use of the compass, and its siting in the middle of the earth's largest land-mass can hardly be by accident.

But mathematics and proportions were, to the ancients, never the purely secular matter they have become to us. They demonstrated the oneness of Creation, and its purpose. And if the interior design of this pyramid is studied, it seems to indicate with its corridors two paths, one ascending steeply upwards with a huge block that must somehow be surmounted before the awe-inspiring Grand Gallery leads into the "King's Chamber", the other descending easily downwards into the very bowels of the earth. well below the pyramid's ground level.. Soon after entering the initiate in its Mysteries must choose which way to go. Was this designed for initiation? Does the great block represent an inadequate level of consciousness? But even if the easy downward corridor is taken, all hope is not lost for there is a rough and almost vertical chimney, very difficult to climb, but offering a last-chance escape even from this nether pit. A third corridor, leading horizontally to the "Queen's Chamber" could on this reading represent a certain stable level of orthodox respectability - but ultimately a dead end from which those desiring to rise higher must retrace their steps.

In view of the awe-inspiring degree of knowledge demonstrated by the facts given above, to say nothing of the consummate level of organisation and craftsmanship displayed in the moving and accurate shaping of the pyramid's huge blocks of stone - does the concept of terrestrial Zodiacs not become a little easier to entertain?

It is not as if such wonders were confined to ancient Egypt; they can be matched in Mexico and the adjacent lands of South America, where the knowledge of Astrology is equally evident. Colossal Avebury and Stonehenge are even earlier..The question of how these Zodiacs came to be, however, is a vexed one, and beyond Katharine Maltwood's belief that the Glastonbury circle was developed by Sumerians, here in search of precious metals, I can only speculate. By its very size and the fact that three of its signs are clearly contoured by hills, it would seem that it has a natural basis. Such effigies as the Fish-shaped Wearyall Hill of Pisces and the two hills of Dundon and Lollover that make the northern Gemini figure could have been recognised from the ground by these merchant-adventurers, who being well versed in Astrology, could have seized on the contours of the Avalon site as a providential one for developing the rest of the pattern. This they could have done by developing settlements at nodal points, which would produce intercommunicating tracks that delineated those parts of the effigies not already drawn by natural streams. The huge Piscean Whale is made by canals extended from the river Brue; and as its discoverer points out, Sumerians were great irrigators of their marshes of Kengi, between the mouths of the Euphrates and Tigris. They could also have reared earth-banks to govern the unruly river Parret that draws the underside of the circle's guardian Hound.

It is the main waterway leading inland to the Glastonbury Zodiac from the Severn, and Mrs. Maltwood reminds us that Sumerian Gilgamesh sailed up the river Parutti, (a remarkably similar name), in his long westward quest for the Mysteries of eternal life.

Such earthworks are certainly on a huge scale - but one only has only to look at the great terraces round the Tor to see that work of these dimensions was undoubtedly going on in the locality; and though no-one is sure of their date, they are typical of the late Neolithic and early Bronze Age.

The Kingston Zodiac has none of these vast earthworks to show, but its circle is even larger - being governed by the winding curves of the Thames, which draws a sizeable amount of the effigies' outlines. As these figures are so similar to those of the Glastonbury Zodiac one can't help wondering whether they are not a copy of Somerset's original. The numinous interpretation they offer is substantially the same, despite certain changes due to the different terrain. Glastonbury's Taurus for instance has only room for its head, while the Thames insists on an enormous Bull, drawing not only its facial profile, but the whole of its underside - while the Kingston boat is smaller than its Glastonbury original, whose extensive Sedgemoor marshes west of Gemini's hills gave the designers plenty of room for making the Cancerian ship's planks by irrigation rhynes.

Such undertakings in both terrestrial Zodiacs must imply the use of accurate maps in very early times, and this preposterous idea makes historians and archaeologists smile. But have they forgotten the mystery contained in the Pirie Reis chart? Though its existing copy is no earlier than the 15th century, this Portuguese sailors' map shows an astonishing knowledge of continents on both sides of the Atlantic, and must have been copied from far earlier sources no longer extant, *for it shows Antarctica as a continent almost free of ice.* And when geologists drilled recently for the original coastline beneath the present Antarctic ice-cap they found substantially the same shape delineated as on the Portuguese copy. Nor is this the only example; Hapgood's "*Maps of the Ancient Sea-Kings*" illustrates several others. Are they copies of Phoenician sailors' maps, copied by them in their turn from even earlier originals? Columbus it seems was not labouring under the delusion that the earth was flat, but sailing for the New World with charts derived from ancestors who not only knew that it was round, but had navigated and mapped it aeons before his time.

Some such explanation of Terrestrial Zodiacs offered in preceding paragraphs is the nearest one to "common sense," and is certainly strengthened by these recent discoveries of our early ancestors' hitherto under-rated capacities.

But how to account for the strangely Zodiacal character of the effigies in both Zodiacs?

To summarise but a few; consider the world-famous and unfailing Spring at Glastonbury's Chalice well, as if poured out by the Water-Carrier Phoenix himself, and the spectacular Tor itself, that so prominently expresses the Aquarian resurrection of the New year. Or the three Water signs of that Zodiac, so low-lying and liable to floods. Or rocky Hurcot Hill whose natural contours draw Leo's head so accurately that they improve on the Mrs. Maltwood's somewhat canine outlines. Or the contrasting mild and verdant terrain of Virgo, whose cows' milk, collected at Wincanton, supplies all London.

The essentially Zodiacal character that marks each Kingston effigy out from the next has already been demonstrated in detail in this book, so I need only repeat one or two examples here. Compare the sharp character-contrast between royal Sagittarius of Richmond/ Kew, and Brentford/Acton's workaday Capricorn - or the martial aspect of Aries' Hounslow Heath compared with the relaxed Venusian charm of the neighbouring area under Taurus.

Such character contrasts recur throughout these effigies, and seem to demand an explanation beyond mere common sense. We can hardly put these down to the labours of our early forbears, however perceptive they may have been - for many of these differences are still developing, as if to some mysterious plan.

Then there are the significant place-names; Avalon's circle has about a hundred of these, and many legends that fit the effigies - notable among them those of Arthur and his knights. Names like Wagg on the Great Dog of Langport and Earlake Moor on his ear may well be ancient memories, for his figure is plain to see on the Somerset map, and beside some twenty-three other name-pointers, he is remembered in the old Wassail song as the "Girt Dog of Langport who burnt his long tail." But some names on the Kingston Zodiac are equally intriguing, though unlikely to be so old.

Spankers Wood in Richmond Park near the rumps of both the Sagittarian rider and his horse, and Pen Ponds on his penis have the explosively funny quality of the unconscious. The Star and Garter near his knee, an old tavern before the Soldiers' Home replaced it, can hardly have been as old as all that.

Phoenix Way, so near the Aquarian Bird, is positively modern. And though it no doubt remembers Heston's aerodrome, its placing here is curiously apt. A third fish has recently appeared in Pisces, its underside drawn by the Grand Union Canal, as if to compensate for the recent northward continuation of Parkway, that has marred the tail of the Cranford Fish.. Railways sometimes help to draw the effigies' outlines, though I have resisted using them. Are some of those human developments unwittingly obeying an unsuspected plan?

Another possible explanation for these Zodiacs is strictly for those with New-Age leanings. I have read somewhere - (Jung?) that "Astrology is one of the treasury vaults of the collective Unconscious." The profound truths of this ancient art can only be fully appreciated by those who really study and experience it for themselves, but to those that do, it begins to appear as yet another of the superhuman wonders of the ancient world.

I would like to suggest here that Zodiacs are a space-time concept; a diagram of the tools of Creation - and thus its effects should be discernible both on Time and Space, or form. The sequential action of its signs can be seen on all time-scales, from the changing character of the vast Precessional Ages, (a cycle of nearly 26000 years), to the yearly seasons, even to down to the daily hours, minutes and seconds used by astrologers in calculating horoscopes.

On the Precessional scale human history only reaches back to about four of these. But count back from today's dawning Aquarian Age, allowing 2160 years for each age to see their changing characteristics. The Piscean Age has been one of mystical faith, often marred (like the two fish tugging in opposite directions), by religious wars. It has built awe-inspiring cathedrals, and fervent missionaries have spread their faiths abroad in the wake of sailors founding successive empires overseas. Early in the Piscean Age, St Paul's sea-journeys spread Christianity all over the Middle East, and the first sign for that faith was not the cross, but the Fishes. Mahomet's teachings took off as the second decanate of Pisces began, about 700 AD; and this decanate, ruled by the moon, is symbolised by the Mohammedan Crescent.

Typically, much of the preceding period of Aries is called the Iron Age, a time for roving warriors like Alexander, pioneers carving out land for themselves with the sword, and decimating the preceding civilisations of the Taurean Age. In the transition from the Taurean to the Arian Age, Moses significantly condemned Bull worship (the Golden Calf) and substituted the sign of the Passover Lamb, calling his faithful to prayer with the Ram's horn.

The Taurean Age was characterised by solid, settled cultures that produced megaliths, mighty earthworks such as Carnac, Avebury and Stonehenge, and the magnificent temples and pyramids of Egypt and Chaldea. Human historical records begin here. Preceding Ages, Geminian and Cancerian, are lost in myth, but it is significant that legends of the Deluge bring us to the Cancerian Age (c.8800-6400BC) of watery inundations on a vast scale. Britain was finally cut off from the continent of Europe by the slowly widening English Channel at this mesolithic period, and has legends recalling the loss of large western tracts of land like Lyonesse, the lost land of Ys and Cardigan Bay. Plato's date for the sinking of Atlantis, about 9400 BC, is only 600 years before the Cancerian Age began, though this takes it back, if he was right, into the last years of the Precessional Age of Leo.

Can it be said that Leo's "Golden Age" (c 10960-8800 BC) dimly remembers the glories of Atlantis, cut short by this disaster?

But here we are in the realms of myth... Coming back to the historical present, it is notable that the last epoch of the Piscean age developed canals and water-power, and this boiled into steam-power and finally to the use of electricity under the looming lightning-rod of Uranus, ruler of the approaching Aquarian Age. New visions of the Brotherhood of Man - a sense of debt to the Third World, of racial equality and the liberation of women, are struggling to come to birth under this emerging Aquarian "Age of the Common Man." The United Nations struggle to realise global justice under the lofty if more secular idealism of friendly Aquarius.

If the Zodiacal time-sequence shows so clearly on this scale, may it not be regarded as a compendium of Creative activity?

I have discovered a smaller time-scale on which this theory seems to work - but going forward through the Zodiac, not

The Men-an-tol
the Penwith Peninsula, Cornwall.

backward. At the end of my book the "*Glastonbury Zodiac*" I have appended a chapter on "English History Fits the Zodiac" using the scale of one year to a degree (thirty years to one sign) with results that astonished me. It was the suspiciously Zodiacal sequence of the Tudor and Stuart dynasties that first alerted me to its possibilities.

Henry Tudor, owing his claim to the throne through his mother, reigned under maternal Cancer. His son Henry VIII, himself a sun-Cancerian, followed him as the very epitome of Leo's sun-king. And what could be more Virgoan than Elizabeth the Virgin Queen? In fact, there were four queens in this period. James I's ambiguous sexuality seems to suit Libra, whose sign tends to equalise the sexes. It was under Libra's Venusian ray that Shakespeare flourished, and the Authorised King James Bible, in style so superior to modern versions, was written. Under Scorpio comes Charles I's outdated assumption of his Divine Right to rule, his execution and Cromwell's ensuing dictatorship. Charles II's reign, libertine yet philosophical, are typically Sagittarian.

When I finally put this theory to the acid test of a mathematical time-scale, not only did these kings and queens fit neatly into their Zodiacal periods, but working back from 1500 on the thirty-year scale I found the little princes in the Tower coming under Gemini - as well as the fighting brothers of the Wars of the Roses. Richard the Lion-Heart and his Scottish contemporary William the Lion both came under a Leo period; William Rufus typified the worst of Taurus, and his father William the Conqueror invaded under Aries' martial sign.

Working forward from the Stuarts proved no less rewarding; George III "Farmer George" comes under a period of Taurus; Victoria became Mother of Millions of her sea-borne Empire during Cancer's maternal water-sign; her son Edward VII presiding regally over another period of Leonine splendour, until Leo's too-arrogant sun set in the blood of the first World War. To bring this calendar up to date, one must hope that Prince Charles, embroiled at present in thirty years of Scorpio, (1980-2010) - fares better than his ill-fated ancestor. These are but a few time-correspondences that appeared, and as the whole theory has already been published, they must suffice here.

If the astrological effects on Time are so evident, its influences on space and form should also be perceptible, for scientists have shown that space and time are indissoluble aspects of the same continuum. And Astrology has traditionally laid down physical as well as psychological characteristics for each Zodiacal type. In fact a good astrologer can often identify your sun-sign and rising sign by your appearance alone. Whole countries have had one Zodiacal sign or other allotted to them by tradition. Is it then so far-fetched to think that these influences could be imprinted on the earth itself in the form of Zodiacs? Katharine Maltwood said that it is as if the stars had kissed the earth, leaving their reflection; and it is notable that these earth-Zodiacs are printed backwards, mirror-like, on the ground, compared with those in star-books. Interestingly, the Celts' favourite oath began " though the stars should fall upon the earth - ".

But whether this is the way of it, or whether these Star-temples were developed by astrologically-preoccupied men in the past, recognising favourable tracts of land and developing their natural potential, I am unable to say. They certainly traced the pattern on the stars, and it may well be they were helped by Jung's Collective Unconscious, or divine inspiration, here.

Although astronomers assert that these figures in the sky are unrecognisable, perhaps it is because they only put one eye to their telescopes that they fail to identify a perfectly good Lion, Virgin or Scorpion when they see one. The V-shaped stars of

Taurus equally suggest the Bull's head, and the magi only needed a few recognisable signs in the right order to complete the pattern. It is true that the other constellations on the Zodiac belt are not so identifiable, but contemporary star-maps do not help to us to recognise those that are, for they often connect up the stars in the wrong order, like bewildered children faced with those puzzle dots in their drawing-books. It takes two eyes, or two brains, both left and right working in intuitive harmony, to see these star-patterns aright.

Are these star-patterns, however they were made, not the thumb-print of the Creator? Indeed, as with all great art, the very style betrays the artist. Not only are they superhuman in scale and their embedded mathematical proportions profound; but the endless sequential interweaving of their signs and planets allows for every possible character-variation, and envisages every possible response to every conceivable situation that can arise.

These figures also tell a story - an autobiography - that reveals the nature of the Artist, His pangs and triumphs in the continuing process of creation. In this process we, as creators on our own microcosmic level, are invited to share, each according to our growing capacity for consciousness. It has something to say to all levels, this story of the suffering Creator that can wring tears both from children and the wise. And no matter how far we grow in understanding, there will always be astrological chapters beyond our comprehension. The story of the loving sun-king, dying ceaselessly to give us life, is the pattern given by Evolution for us to follow - for we ourselves are embryonic sun-kings in the making.

A strange pattern indeed, that allows for - even demands - our free-will. A vast jigsaw, incomplete until every piece has found its true place by trial and error. Yet if we are slow learners, what else is Time for?

All things both great and small are comprehended in this vast clock. On it each of us may read our individual horoscope and learn our part in the Cosmic Scheme; what we must do, and undo - who we are, from whence, where we are going, and why....

FREE DETAILED CATALOGUE

Fairies in the Irish Tradition, Molly Gowen
Familiars - Animal Powers of Britain, Anna Franklin
Fool's First Steps, (The) Chris Thomas
Forest Paths - Tree Divination, Brian Harrison, Ill. S. Rouse
From Past to Future Life, Dr Roger Webber
Gardening For Wildlife Ron Wilson
God Year, The, Nigel Pennick & Helen Field
Goddess on the Cross, Dr George Young
Goddess Year, The, Nigel Pennick & Helen Field
Goddesses, Guardians & Groves, Jack Gale
Handbook For Pagan Healers, Liz Joan
Handbook of Fairies, Ronan Coghlan
Healing Book, The, Chris Thomas and Diane Baker
Healing Homes, Jennifer Dent
Healing Stones, Sue Philips
Herb Craft - Shamanic & Ritual Use of Herbs, Lavender & Franklin
Hidden Heritage - Exploring Ancient Essex, Terry Johnson
In Search of Herne the Hunter, Eric Fitch
Intuitive Journey, Ann Walker Isis - African Queen, Akkadia Ford
Journey Home, The, Chris Thomas
Kecks, Keddles & Kesh - Celtic Lang & The Cog Almanac, Bayley
Legend of Robin Hood, The, Richard Rutherford-Moore
Lid Off the Cauldron, Patricia Crowther
Light From the Shadows - Modern Traditional Witchcraft, Gwyn
Living Tarot, Ann Walker
Lore of the Sacred Horse, Marion Davies
Lost Lands & Sunken Cities (2nd ed.), Nigel Pennick
Magic of Herbs - A Complete Home Herbal, Rhiannon Ryall
Magical Guardians - Exploring the Spirit and Nature of Trees, Philip Heselton
Magical History of the Horse, Janet Farrar & Virginia Russell
Magical Lore of Animals, Yvonne Aburrow
Magical Lore of Cats, Marion Davies
Magical Lore of Herbs, Marion Davies
Magick Without Peers, Ariadne Rainbird & David Rankine
Masks of Misrule - Horned God & His Cult in Europe, Nigel Jackson
Medicine For The Coming Age, Lisa Sand MD
Medium Rare - Reminiscences of a Clairvoyant, Muriel Renard
Mind Massage - 60 Creative Visualisations, Marlene Maundrill
Mirrors of Magic - Evoking the Spirit of the Dewponds, P Heselton
Moon Mysteries, Jan Brodie
Mysteries of the Runes, Michael Howard
Mystic Life of Animals, Ann Walker
Pagan Feasts - Seasonal Food for the 8 Festivals, Franklin & Phillips
Patchwork of Magic - Living in a Pagan World, Julia Day
Pathworking - A Practical Book of Guided Meditations, Pete Jennings
Pillars of Tubal Cain, Nigel Jackson

Places of Pilgrimage and Healing, Adrian Cooper
Practical Divining, Richard Foord
Practical Spirituality, Steve Hounsome
Psychic Self Defence - Real Solutions, Jan Brodie
Real Fairies, David Tame
Reality - How It Works & Why It Mostly Doesn't, Rik Dent
Romany Tapestry, Michael Houghton
Runic Astrology, Nigel Pennick
Sacred Animals, Gordon MacLellan
Sacred Celtic Animals, Marion Davies, Ill. Simon Rouse
Sacred Dorset - On the Path of the Dragon, Peter Knight
Sacred Grove - The Mysteries of the Forest, Yvonne Aburrow
Sacred Geometry, Nigel Pennick
Sacred Nature, Ancient Wisdom & Modern Meanings, A Cooper
Sacred Ring - Pagan Origins of British Folk Festivals, M. Howard
Seasonal Magic - Diary of a Village Witch, Paddy Slade
Secret Places of the Goddess, Philip Heselton
Secret Signs & Sigils, Nigel Pennick
Self Enlightenment, Mayan O'Brien
Spirits of the Air, Jaq D Hawkins
Spirits of the Earth, Jaq D Hawkins
Spirits of the Earth, Jaq D Hawkins
Stony Gaze, Investigating Celtic Heads John Billingsley
Subterranean Kingdom, The, revised 2nd ed, Nigel Pennick
Symbols of Ancient Gods, Rhiannon Ryall
The Other Kingdoms Speak, Helena Hawley
Tree: Essence of Healing, Simon & Sue Lilly
Tree: Essence, Spirit & Teacher, Simon & Sue Lilly
Understanding Chaos Magic, Jaq D Hawkins
Water Witches, Tony Steele
West Country Wicca, Rhiannon Ryall
Wildwitch - The Craft of the Natural Psychic, Poppy Palin
Wildwood King , Philip Kane
Witches of Oz, Matthew & Julia Philips
Wondrous Land - The Faery Faith of Ireland by Dr Kay Mullin